Planning The Perfect Asian Wedding

VENTURE PUBLISHING
INTERNATIONAL

ISBN-13: 978-1470105891

ISBN-10: 1470105896

Cover Photograph © Lijuan Guo

Printed in U.S.A

DEDICATION

This book is dedicated to all of the incredible
professionals and companies who took the time
to submit content for this book and for sharing
their individual expertise in their field.

CONTENTS

Acknowledgments

Introduction   1

1   Food for all tastes – Hiring the ideal   3
Wedding Caterer

2   Classic to contemporary – Fabulous flowers   8
for your wedding

3   Wedding cakes as individual as you are   16

4   Arriving in style - Wedding Cars fit for the   22
occasion

5   Making your mark - Invitations for your   28
special day

6   Hiring a Live band - Your perfect wedding   37
entertainment

7   The First Dance - Getting it right on your   43
big day

8   Getting Into The Groove – Hiring The Right   53
Wedding DJ

9   Henna - Adding the magic touch to your Big   59
Day

10   Stylish to the sophisticated - Creating your   67
perfect wedding dress

11   Looking radiant on your big day – Finding   74
the right Make-up artist

12 Professional or contemporary - The right   88
    photographer for your wedding

13 Unique, elegant and affordable – Choosing   96
    the right bridal Jeweller

14 Capturing your day in style with the right   107
    videographer

15 Planning your ideal day with the help of a   113
    Toastmaster

    Conclusion   119

ACKNOWLEDGMENTS

With Special Thanks To:

Poonams Caterers & Event Coordinators
Todich Floral Designs
Halal Cakes 4U
JD Prestige Cars
Ananya: without equal
Eastern Illusion Ltd
Honeys Dance Academy
Sensation Entertainments
Mehndi Creations
Inspiration Couture
Karishma, Hair & Makeup
Tapas Maiti Photography
Pure Jewels
JSV Media
The London Toastmaster

INTRODUCTION

South Asian weddings are very bright colourful events celebrated in a much more lavish and magnificent way than Western weddings. Filled with ritual and celebration that will often continue for several days South Asian Weddings are generally not small affairs, with anywhere between 100 to 10,000 people attending. Organizing such a wedding can be a daunting task; there is just so much to be done, so many different parts of the wedding to get ready, that sometimes it can be overwhelming even when everything goes according to plan. To overcome the many problems associated with organising an Asian wedding, and to turn a potential nightmare into a dream, really does only take one thing – *expert planning from people who know what they are doing*.

Weddings can often be the subject of funny stories for the guests. These same "funny stories", however, are usually nightmares or unpleasant events for the bride and groom. In the great majority of cases, these unpleasant incidences could have been avoided if the bride and groom had just a little bit of "insider knowledge" when they were planning their wedding. The very nature of most weddings, however, is that it's a first-time and often one-time event, where there are no second chances. The best strategy for getting it right the first time, therefore, is to learn from the experts who have years of experience in the wedding industry.

Planning The Perfect Asian Wedding is a compilation of vital information that you absolutely must have before you embark on the massive task of planning your own wedding. Our interviewees have shared their knowledge and expertise, to help your wedding go off without a hitch. When we set out to publish this book, it was our goal to obtain real world, usable advice, from true industry experts. We are proud to tell you that we have exceed even our own expectations, in this regard.

Very often, in books that are written in this interview style, you will find interviews with professionals who are mainly just interested in promoting their own companies. We are pleased to let you know that the contributors of this book have truly put your interests ahead of their own. As you will see, from reading these interviews, each of our contributors shares exactly what you need to do and what you need to avoid doing when you're planning your wedding.

Married couples will often look back on their wedding day, wishing they had done certain things differently. After reading this book, the likelihood of you having those same regrets will be greatly diminished. Your wedding is truly a milestone event in your life and we set out to ensure that you get it right the first time, because hopefully, there won't be a second time! No matter the situation, one of our experienced interviewees has been there before, and they have graciously taken the time to offer their advice to ensure that you don't hit the same wedding snags that they have witnessed countless others make. We genuinely believe that after reading Planning The Perfect Asian Wedding you will feel confident to plan your wedding with enthusiasm and certainty. So, without further ado, let's get into the interviews!

1.
FOOD FOR ALL TASTES – HIRING THE IDEAL WEDDING CATERER

Poonams is a well reputed company and has been established since 1976. It stemmed from within the community, grew with it and established itself within it and beyond. Our client base extends itself from those we cater for at wedding related functions, to those that indulge in our food and distribute our sweets at other celebrations, aeroplane passengers that enjoy our snacks and desserts and everyday customers that buy snacks on their way to work and sweets on their way to the temple. We are delighted to organise occasions from start to finish and alleviate all the stresses and strains from our clients. We assist our clients in their venue search, creating the perfect menu, deciding on reception decor and composing an itinerary for their big day. Having been established for 35 years, we take pride in our adaptability and versatility in this ever-growing Asian wedding industry.

What information do caterers typically need from a couple prior to hiring them for a wedding?

A couple would need to provide a minimum number of guests in order to provide an accurate quotation. As there are many variations within Asian cuisine it is useful to discuss the type of cuisine required, e.g. Punjabi, South Indian, Gujarati etc. It is important to note any specific dietary requirements, for example does the meat need to be Halal? Also let your caterer

3

know if they need to exclude any specific ingredients like onion and or garlic etc. A couple should consider the type of service they require for example, a complete table service or buffet service. Location of the event is also very important information a caterer needs so that they can determine what travel costs are involved and what facilities are available to them at a particular venue.

How soon before a wedding do caterers normally need a final headcount?

I would advise going through every detail at least four weeks prior to the wedding date. This gives you time to enjoy the lead up to your wedding knowing that the majority of the work is done. Although it may vary between caterers, we at Poonams allow for changes to be made up to 7 working days prior to the wedding date. This gives us just enough time to adjust our function sheets accordingly and alert any other suppliers that we may be using.

How soon before a wedding does the bride or groom need to finalise the menu?

I recommend doing this at least four weeks prior to the wedding date although check with your individual caterer about this. We allow for menu changes to be made up to 7 working days prior to the wedding date. It is nice to have a few weeks in between to reflect on the choices you have made so that you feel satisfied with them.

Can caterers arrange a food tasting prior to hiring them? Is there a fee for a sample tasting?

Most, if not all caterers do conduct food tasters. Some may charge a small fee and elsewhere it may be complimentary. Where a fee is charged, this may be refunded if and when a booking is confirmed.

What are some of the different types of cuisines Asian Wedding Caterers offer and how do caterers handle certain religious and dietary restrictions?

The wonderful thing about Asian cuisine is that it covers so many different tastes. There are also different geographical variations to consider, for example Punjabi cuisine, Gujarati cuisine, South Indian cuisine. And then there are religious variations to consider, for example Muslims require halal meat, some Hindu's require food prepared with no onion or garlic etc. The Asian palette is wide and varied.

In general do caterers prepare food on-site or is it brought in ready?

In most cases, all curries are cooked in the caterers own kitchens and reheated on-site. Items that can be fried are usually fried fresh on-site. In some cases with the permission of the venue, caterers are able to take a tandoor on site to make fresh naan bread. However this option usually incurs an extra charge as the tandoor itself needs to be transported to the venue and extra staff need to be arranged.

How long does it take to set up and to break down an event?

The set up and break down time of an event will vary according to the size and specific requirements of each event. Generally speaking, to set up for 500 guests we allow 4 hours to set up and it usually takes 60 – 90 minutes to break down an event and leave the kitchens and the event room in a satisfactory condition.

Do caterers normally provide waiters? If so, what is the customary server-to-guest ratio?

Your caterer should be able to provide waiters for your event. The server to guest ration will vary with the level of service booked. Generally we would recommend a 1:20 ratio. This ratio is purely for food service and does not include service of alcoholic beverages.

Do caterers normally cut and serve the wedding cake?

Caterers don't usually mind cutting and serving the wedding cake. Just remember to leave instructions on when and how you would like your cake served.

What are some other things that a bride or groom generally need to rent with catering services?

All essential service items are usually included within the quote, e.g. service bowls for curries. Other items generally booked with caterers are cutlery, crockery, linen, glassware, table number stands, karahi stands and lazy susans (rotating tray).

What is usually done with the leftover food?

Caterers discard the leftover food. The reason you can't take leftover food is food safety and our liability. It is dangerous to eat food that has dropped below certain temperature when it's been sitting out for hours. At an event you have a good few hours between food service and the end of the event and there isn't usually enough space or time to store the food properly.

Typically, how much deposit is needed and when is the final balance due?

Check this with your individual caterer, but about 20% is usually a reasonable amount to pay as a deposit. The final balance must be cleared prior to the event.

What are some other important points a couple should consider when hiring a caterer for their wedding?

We believe that 'reliability' and 'quality' are the two things to keep in mind when looking for a caterer. It is best to find a caterer that offers some form of event management for your day. This will amongst many things include discussing your itinerary so that service times can be established and appointing a point of contact from your side so that any changes to the itinerary (which isn't uncommon at Asian weddings!) can be authorised by someone you trust to make decisions on your part

---

HOW TO CONTACT US

Poonams Caterers Bookings and Enquiries:
Website: www.poonams.com
Email: shikha@poonams.com
Telephone: +44 (0)20 8813 9300
Mobile: +44 (0)7852 123 610
Facebook: Like us on Facebook

2.
CLASSIC TO CONTEMPORARY –
FABULOUS FLOWERS FOR YOUR WEDDING

Todich Floral Design is an award winning wedding and event's florist that has a highly skilled and creative team of managers, experts and florists who are passionate about flowers, having been in business for over 15 years; Todich Floral Design has built up an exceptional reputation with both clients and contracts. Based in South London, We provide a bespoke bridal flower service throughout all of London and the south east of England. From ceremony to reception our flowers create the perfect mood for a bride's big day, we are proud to say that we treat each of our happy couples with the best client service. One of the most important days of a couple's life deserves an expert florist's attention and planning. Attempting to blend artistry & elegance with our own innovation, We produce high quality designs on a daily basis, Our aim is to turn floral dreams into reality, our florists create fresh, innovative, contemporary arrangements which keeps bringing clients back over and over again. *Finalist - Florist of the Year Award 2009.*

What should couples be aware of when selecting a florist for their big day?

Nothing ties your wedding together quite like your wedding flowers, so it is vital that the florist you book is the right one for you and your style. Good florists get booked up quickly; therefore it is essential that you look for the right florist as early into your wedding plans as possible. We recommend you meet your chosen florist in person, take a note of the their website and style, Ask yourself - do they look like they are bursting with fresh ideas or that they have been stuck in a rut for the last 10 years?, If first impressions are good, ask to see the florist's portfolio, paying particular attention to past weddings that they have worked on. Couples should also be aware that it is important for the florist to know how much that you are willing to spend; this should be discussed in the first consultation, and that the florist can then recommend designs within your price range. Know what you want, don't feel obliged to book anyone there and then. If you need more time to make your decision, just say so. A good florist should understand how important it is to choose the right person. Lastly ask for a contract – Before you sign make sure you receive a written quotation. This should clearly list the prices that you have requested in the consultations. Once you are happy with this should you enter into a contract with them, when you have confirmed your order, you'll probably be asked to pay a deposit, with the final balance due a few weeks before the big day. Bear in mind that if you change your mind about the flowers you want or the number of arrangements you require in the run-up of the wedding day, this could affect your final bill.

What are some simple things that a couple can do to ensure that their flowers are consistent with what they visualized for their wedding?

It is recommended that couples should take the time to identify the central, personal theme of their wedding, as this can shape the decorative style of the whole day. For some brides, their theme may be a colour, a piece of music or era, while for others it may be jewellery or vintage. Once the bride has found her theme and costumed her wedding to this style, it can become very inspiring for the florist. Many brides are consistent with the theme throughout the wedding from the bridesmaid's dresses down to the stationary and furnishings, putting a scrapbook together of your theme including colours and fabric samples will make this a much easier visual display for the florist to match the flowers within your wedding venue.

Can wedding bouquets be customized or can only certain flowers be used in bouquets?

The wonderful thing about flowers is that there are hardly restrictions; with a huge variety of colours, styles and flowers, there is a diverse range for brides all year around. Most flowers are available all year, obviously there are a few exceptions and fluctuations in prices depending on the time of year you marry, but a good florist should always find a way to work around these issues, either by stating the flowers availability in the first few consultations or by substituting to a similar alike flower. The time of year can also help set your theme. For example, spring brides could go for scented pink and whites peony's, freesias and sweet peas, whilst those having a summer wedding might decide to go for a bouquet of sunflowers, gerberas and still grass, In autumn, we would suggest zantesdeschia's, coffee break roses and twigs in spicy vibrant colours. And in winter, look for sumptuous flowers in deeps colours such as crimson tulips and violet anemones Your bouquet can always be customised to your taste, if you are after a classical period bouquet then It is the attention to minor details that is important in creating this style, accessorising is key, and incorporating diamantes, pearls, brooches and velvet ribbon can made your flowers stand out and be a beautiful unique design.

What is the customary process for placing deposits and paying the remaining balance?

At Todich floral design, you simply pay a 20% deposit to secure you wedding day with us. This way the whole day is solely devoted to you, we understand the emotions for the perfect wedding with every bride which is why we pledge to provide you with the best service possible. We arrange only your flowers and aim to make sure that the flowers are perfect for your wedding day. The remaining balance is due a month prior to the wedding, this is so that we can reserve your chosen flowers in advance, as well as order in any accessories if required from the discussed consultations.

How do Asian wedding florals differ from English wedding florals?

The flowers of an Asian wedding tend to predominantly be bright, vibrant colours; a mix of oranges, reds and yellows seems to be the main theme, bright and beautiful is the key. Gold spayed foliage leaves are frequently requested. Asian bride's often do not hold a bouquet but instead the bride, groom and guests wear colourful garlands. The wedding party is usually much larger and more table flower arrangements are required. The flowers of an English wedding are dependent on season. Spring and summer weddings are always most popular due to the weather and the beautiful flower varieties you can choose from at this time of year. Traditionally bouquets consist of white and one other simple colour, however now, vibrant splashes of colours such as a bouquet of sunflowers and cerise gerberas seem to be an up and coming modern trend.

Are the flowers for the ceremony and the wedding reception two separate orders or are they typically all ordered as one package?

The flowers for the wedding ceremony and reception are treated as one order as it is all written in one quote, we however do dispatch separately as we would have discussed with you in the consultations.

How far in advance should couples order their wedding flowers?

It is best to book your florist as soon as possible to avoid disappointment. We at Todich floral design only every take one wedding a week, as it's important for us to be able to give time and energy to each bride's wedding flowers. One year before the wedding date we recommend the happy couple compile a scrap book of ideas, this way determining a theme, colour and style of the day; this will give the florist enough inspiration to match the flowers to your style. As a rule of thumb, we recommend discussing flowers with your florist once the dress has been chosen.

Considering that weddings take place on specific times and dates, how can a couple ensure that wedding flowers are delivered at the right time, for the ceremony and the reception?

Keep in touch with your florist, arrange plenty of consultations, and make sure your florist has a list of emergency contact numbers. 3 days before the wedding, check that the florist had ordered all the flowers. Always make sure that all important information is in writing confirming both florist and the clients and mutual agreement. Most florists set up three hours before the ceremony, so couples must plan a suitable schedule, we recommend that couples double check with the venue that the florists will be able to set up at a pre-arranged time.

Is it fairly common for couples to meet with the florist prior to their wedding? If so, what should a couple bring with them to a consultation?

It is very common for couples to meet up with the florist; we always arrange more than one consultation with future brides so that we can develop a relationship and an understanding to exactly what you wish, the florists at Todich floral design truly believe that the most important thing about the initial consultation is the rapport. Prior to the consultations we recommend that every bride should put together a scrap book of ideas. Gathering favourite images of flower varieties from magazines and the internet is a great way for brides to find what they do and don't like. We advise adding photographs of your chosen venue in the scrapbook as this will also help us and you determine the looks you are after.

When you have chosen your wedding and bridesmaid's dresses, build to your scrapbook, treat it like a mood board, creating pictures of your dress, adding fabric samples and different textures to create more inspiration for your big day. Your scrapbook will be your guide to your favourite colours and flowers. If like many brides; you do not have a scrapbook prepared then we at Todich Floral Design are always happy to spend time showing our portfolio of past weddings in our consultations. It is always helpful if you tell the florist as much information as possible, we would love to hear about your dreams for your big day and what you would like to achieve.

Approximately how much should a couple budget for their flowers, in proportion to their entire wedding budget?

Approximately 10-15%, we always ask about your budget at the very first meeting, as it's extremely important to agree on how much we are working with before starting on the design concept. We will then try to accommodate the design agreed within that budget, and when the proposal is accepted, we stick firmly to the budget unless any further additions are requested by you. A bridal bouquet should cost anything from £45.00 upwards. A really simple bouquet shouldn't cost an arm and a leg but, equally, a bride who wants local English flowers should be prepared to pay as much, or more, than a conventional bouquet.

Is it true that flower prices fluctuate throughout the year? If so, by how much do these prices fluctuate?

It is very true that flower prices fluctuate throughout the year. Dependant on the flower's season they can increase rather dramatically by about 80%. Roses at valentines almost treble in price and the beautiful spring flower peony can almost half in price as the height of their season. Peony's only lasts for 4 weeks, which makes them very difficult to get hold of for the rest of the year. Couples should try to take seasonality into account when deciding on their wedding flowers. The florists at Todich Floral Design suggest that couples pick varieties of flowers that will be at the height of their season around the date of their wedding. This way, you will find that the flowers will be particularly stunning and fresh, and your budget will stretch that little bit further. We however warn that brides should be cautious of choosing their wedding date over busy public holidays; florists are very busy around Mother's day, Valentine's Day and Christmas, which means flower prices will always cost more at these times.

What else should a couple consider when selecting a florist for their wedding day?

Couples should feel confident and trust their instincts, if you feel you are on the right wavelength with your florist then this is a good start. Don't feel pressured to spend over your budget but be open to new floral designs and ideas; Give the florist a chance to share different and even unusual designs with you. Sticking to one type of flower and one style can often limit creativity and flexibility with different styles. We find that 90% of the time, when a bride is shown a completely different arrangement, they fall in love and this is often the one they choose.

HOW TO CONTACT US

Todich Floral Design Orders and Enquiries:
Shop: Arch 405, Lilford Road, London SE5 9HR.
Telephone: +44 (0)20 7738 4049
Websites: www.todichfloraldesign.co.uk

3.
WEDDING CAKES AS INDIVIDUAL AS YOU ARE

Our Company **Halal Cakes 4U** specializes in Halal and eggless cakes for all occasions. What sets us apart from others is the fact that we thoroughly research our ingredients to make sure that they are completely free from non-halal ingredients which are alcohol and animal or insect extracts. We also ensure that the best branded ingredients are used in the making of our cakes. We spend a lot of time and effort in getting the final result just right, and have built our reputation on the highest quality, taste and hygiene standards. In our first year of business, we have been awarded 5h for hygiene by the Birmingham City Council; this is the highest score possible for hygiene and Management standards. Our passion for making cakes takes priority over business; our designs are tailor made by us, to our customer's requirements and we put in every effort to ensure that the customer is left with a cake to remember for their special occasion.

How long, before the big day, should a wedding cake be ordered?

Ideally, it should be ordered at least 3 weeks in advance, as there is a lot of sourcing of materials the baker has to do. The earlier you book your wedding cake order, the more chance you will have of it being accepted. To guarantee a booking, it would be advised to order as soon as you have information on the wedding date, the design you may discuss and the number of guests the cake will serve. However, depending on what is required, the cake maker may able to fulfill a request for a wedding cake just a matter of days in advance. A bakery may be able to fulfill a wedding cake order a couple of days before, however, keep in mind that a cake specialist is completely different from a bakery as the quality and standard of cake is much higher and the personalisation of your cake will make it a truly individual experience.

What are some factors that determine the various prices of wedding cakes?

There are many factors, for instance, the number of guests to be served will determine the size of the cake. The design, colours, number of tiers required, flavours, the kinds of flowers, ribbons, decorations...the list goes on. It would be helpful to let your cake maker know what your budget is when beginning the consultation, this helps in suggesting what kind of design you can go for. A cake with a lot of intricate design or expensive flowers or one which is more elaborate would cost more. The time it takes to make, assemble and decorate the cake also plays a part in determining the price.

What are some of the different ingredient and flavour options that can be selected for wedding cakes?

Depending on what the bride and groom like, for example, if the wedding is in spring or summer, then you may want to go for refreshing flavours like Lime and Coconut fillings and lemon sponges. This is very varied, from vanilla sponge, fruit cake, to lemon, pistachio, chocolate, strawberries and cream, coffee, in fact, almost any flavour and colour. With regard to ingredients, there are very many choices of cakes, so this would determine the ingredients, for example, if a pistachio cake is required, then pistachios would be required, also a little essence or flavouring which would enhance the mild flavour of pistachios. It may be a good idea to have each tier with different flavours and fillings so all tastes are catered for.

What if a couple want an elaborate wedding cake designed? What information will a cake artist need?

The artist would need to discuss your ideas, ask you what kind of colour scheme will be present in the wedding and what the bride will wear on the day. You should let the artist know what colours and flavours are definitely out and which colours and flavours are a possibility. The artist may even need to take photos of things like the bride's wedding clothes, jewellery and accessories and you may want to bring in photos of ideas to come up with something memorable for your special day. Ideas need to be swapped and bounced around by both the Customer and Artist. Make sure your cake designer can show you how your cake may look by doing a sketch to see if you're happy with it as well and that details are included in the sketch, especially your personal touch, as it makes all the difference to your cake.

Do wedding cake bakers generally allow couples to sample cakes before ordering them? If yes, is there usually a cost for this?

Yes, depending on where you go for samples there is sometimes a cost associated with this, however, it is usually small. Some Cake Makers will also offer a small sample cake, whereas others will offer slices of different flavours so that customers get a good idea of the design, taste and quality and they will know what to expect on the actual day of the wedding.

What special instructions/arrangements can be made to account for people with certain dietary requirements?

You need to mention any special dietary requirements at your consultation. Whether you may have guests who have special requirements like eggless or nut free cakes Depending on this, your Cake Maker will go according to your needs. If there are pre-arranged flowers, that need to be placed on a cake, whom normally does this? Your Cake Maker, or Sugarcraft Specialist who works with them will set flowers on the cake, as it is very often, not as simple as it looks. Flowers normally require some form of attachment to the cake and it is not as straightforward as placing them on a cake. The flowers need to be placed in the correct way and be part of the cake, the angle, the looks; the way they are displayed makes all the difference to the cake which is the centerpiece of your reception.

Do wedding cakes usually include a cake topper, or is this ordered separately?

Depending on what the topper will be, for example, if you're going to have artificial flowers, they will be included with the price. If you want something more extravagant or something which takes a lot of time to make, then your cake maker will charge more.

Who normally puts the cake topper on a wedding cake and when is this done?

Ideally the cake maker does this, as they are most familiar with the design of your wedding cake and how it should be set up. It is very important for your cake maker to be there to do the set up at the venue, that way, they can check that the cake looks the part from every angle. The finishing touch is the cake topper, this is put on last.

What if more people will be attending the wedding than was originally expected? What can be done to ensure that there will be enough cake for these extra guests?

Discuss this at your consultation. If you are not sure how many guests you are having, then maybe it would be good to get a bigger sized cake initially. Another option you can have is to have an extra, separate, single tier cake to serve.

Who is normally responsible for delivering the cake to the reception location?

The Cake Maker is usually the person responsible, as they know how the cake will travel and how it is to be treated during transit, having said this, you may want to pick up the cake on the day, or maybe send someone to pick it up. If this is the case, then the cake maker will instruct you on how to transport the cake and set it up at the venue.

Is a delivery charge standard on wedding cake orders?

Many Cake makers do charge for delivery and it usually is not the same price as a standard cake because there is a lot more responsibility in delivering a wedding cake, for instance it may be a stacked cake. If the reception is close by to us, then we don't charge, but this also depends on how complex the cake is to set up and how close the venue is to us.

How far in advanced are wedding cakes prepared

This depends on the type of cake and the flavours you have chosen. Normally, wedding cakes are completed a day or sometimes two days before the wedding day. The final touches are made to the cake the night before.

Can a couple make changes to a wedding cake after the order has been placed?

Yes that is possible, however, sometimes a cost can be incurred, for example, if a certain item is bought after the deposit is placed, then the customer changes their mind, then the cost would need to be transferred to the customer. It is less likely to be possible if the change request is made towards the date of the wedding, as most materials would have been bought/made already, but if the change request is made very soon after the order is placed, then there is more likelihood of the change happening smoothly and with minimal or no extra cost to you.

HOW TO CONTACT US

Halal Cakes 4u Orders and Enquiries:
Website: www.halalcakes4u.co.uk
Email: info@halalcakes4u.co.uk
Telephone: +44 (0)7877 546 992

4.
ARRIVING IN STYLE -
WEDDING CARS FIT FOR THE OCCASION

JD Prestige Cars is a leading wedding car company in the UK, we specialise in Asian weddings with a range of Chauffeur driven vehicles. So much so that 6 of our vehicles carry variations of V1YAH/V1VAH on our number plates meaning wedding in Punjabi/Hindi/Urdu

What should a couple's budget be for wedding car hire?

The budget for hiring a wedding car depends on the itinerary, locations, dates, duration of hire, and type of vehicle required. We estimate anywhere from £195-£2000. This will include all the petrol, driver, and ribbons.

How far in advance should a couple book their wedding car?

We always recommend 6-9 months in advance especially over the peak season period April - October. Reputable suppliers like us get booked out very quickly over the peak months. We always have clients booking up to 18 months in advance. Also if people book in advance they get a chance to see the vehicles and pick the car they want. Prices tend to be cheaper with earlier bookings too.

Do wedding car hire prices vary, based on when the actual wedding takes place? If so, how does this work?

Yes, if it is a Bank holiday weekend or any weekend between March and September, then prices will vary on demand and supply. There are limited suppliers of wedding cars and a lot more weddings that take place in the peak periods, so demand is high. Off peak prices Nov- Feb mean lower rates as demand is lower. We have now started to do a lot of weekday weddings and the hire rates are cheaper for weekday weddings than a weekend wedding.

Can wedding cars be rented for short periods of time, such as for one hour?

This will vary for each company. We allow a one way drop or a one hour hire but only if we can fit it in a day where we, let's say have an evening wedding or let's say a church wedding in the afternoon and it is local, but otherwise we will have a minimum 3 hour hire. In the off peak season we might have more flexibility so may be able to accommodate shorter trips more readily.

What types of cars are most popular at Asian weddings?

It all depends on the client, JD Prestige Cars for instance does modern vehicles and our flagship model the Rolls Royce Phantom and the Bentley Flying Spur are the most popular models but we get requests for Ambassadors, VW campers and the Route Master Bus. We have even had a request for a Reliant Robin and a lorry without the trailer. Asian weddings tend to be about the "bling" as I say, and many of our clients take 2 or more cars. And many also want a self driver super car like an Aston DB9 or Ferrari.

Can the wedding party bring alcohol into the hired cars?

Nearly all companies won't allow alcohol in the vehicles except in limousines but at the end of the day as long as the clients are respectful we won't say no to the occasional glass of champagne.

What is the dress code for chauffeurs?

Each car hire company is different so it is always best to check with them. At JD Prestige cars all our chauffeurs come suited and booted in a smart black suit, white shirt and black tie and polished shoes. This is highly important, as the image of the company and the driver plays such a major role on the day.

If a wedding needs to be cancelled or re-scheduled, how do most wedding car hire companies handle this?

Most car companies will say you lose your deposit, and if it is near the hire date you may be liable for the whole amount depending on the contract you have signed. At JD Prestige Cars we will carry your deposit over for 12 months and you can re-book with us which works out very favourably with clients as sometimes, the wedding may need to be cancelled for whatever reason.

Approximately how many people can fit in one limousine?

It all depends on the limo you hire and if it is a stretch limo. A lot of people call the Bentley and Rolls Royce a limo which only seat 4 plus driver. A stretch limo will start at 8 seats and can carry all the way up to 20 people depending on the type of limo it is.

Are there any other fees typically associated with a wedding car hire? If there are, please explain these fees.

It depends on the itinerary, if it's a week day and the wedding is in central London you may get charged for the congestion charge. You may also get charged for red carpets and tailor made ribbons but normally if the request doesn't mean us having to pay for additional items it is all inclusive.

Is smoking normally allowed in hired wedding cars?

No, smoking in hire vehicles is not permitted as it is illegal.

What are the normal contingency plans if a car breaks down?

We can't speak for other companies, but we at JD Prestige Cars keep our cars maintained by the main dealers. Yes this costs us a lot of money but they do make sure that the car is running well. If we do have an issue, then we are a company with a number of vehicles and have access to a lot of other vehicles. We would send a like for like replacement as soon as possible.

If the wedding runs longer than expected, who is responsible for the extra time?

We would say that the client is responsible. However, we at JD Prestige Cars understand Asian weddings and know it is not normally the fault of the client but more the whole logistical set up of the day that can cause delays. After all, coordinating 500-600 people in a day is hard work, delays can occur. We normally take that into account and tailor the quote on what the client requires, so most times we are well within the time limits but if they start going over seriously then, we have an hourly rate which is explained to the client at the point of booking.

After the deposit is paid, how soon is the balance normally due?

The balance is normally due 1 week before and most people pay it before, as it is one less worry on the day but we are happy to take payment on the day and we have a number of methods of payment from Credit/Debit card, BACS, CHAPS, and cash to do that.

What other important points should a couple consider when looking for a wedding car hire company?

- Make sure you see the cars. A lot of people boast they have the cars and they don't.

- Make sure you see the actual car you will be getting.

- Make sure the company is reputable, do your homework ask people, ask for testimonials, check reviews, call one of the companies clients.

- If your family have used someone then go with the recommendation as you know what you are in for.

- Make sure there is a contingency plan if things go wrong on the day.

- Make sure you can pay by credit/debit card as that protects your deposit in the event of an issue.

- If your wedding involves a lot of mileage then go for a car that will be comfortable for a long journey.

- When hiring a car make sure the company has public liability.

HOW TO CONTACT US

JD Prestige Cars Bookings and Enquiries:

Website: www.jdprestigecars.com

Email: info@jdprestigecars.com

Telephone: +44 (0)20 8384079

5.
MAKING YOUR MARK -
INVITATIONS FOR YOUR SPECIAL DAY

Ananya is the Sanskrit word for 'without equal' or 'unparalleled'. **Ananya: without equal**, headed by Vaishali Shah has been in business since 2006. We are a luxury, bespoke and boutique design company, creating cards and stationery for significant life events that are distinct, unique and a fusion of Asian and British styles. Our stylish wedding stationery range includes save the date cards, wedding invitations, menus, place cards, table plans, order of service, monograms and thank you cards. Our popular Diwali, Eid, Chinese and Jewish New Year cards give a contemporary interpretation to traditional celebrations. We also cater to the discerning corporate connoisseur with impactful stationery.

Shortlist: Best Brand Campaign, Chartered Institute of Marketing Awards Jersey 2011
Finalist: Creative Business of the Year, Precious Awards

How far in advance should a couple place an order for Wedding Invitations?

Invitations are generally sent between 6 and 8 weeks in advance of the wedding. If it is a destination wedding or there are guests coming from abroad, then you would need to allow more time. For bespoke wedding invitations, the complete process from meeting the client, creating the design and presenting the proof takes between 2 and 3 months. It is a very involved and details oriented process, with many stages until the final result, so the more time you allow the more flexibility there is to make changes and additions.

What is the standard way to make payment for personalized wedding invitations, with regard to deposits and paying the balance?

The standard method of payment is by bank transfer, with a 50% deposit at the start and the remaining 50% upon completion of the contract.

What measures can be taken to ensure that there isn't any spelling, or other typographical errors on the wedding invitations, before they are printed?

We at Ananya are very detail oriented and take great pains not just to make sure there are no spelling mistakes, but that all the details are accurate. The client also checks all the details as well – that way, there is no room for mistakes.

Who actually mails the wedding invitations?

The majority of bridal couples prefer to mail the invitations themselves as they have their list of invitees and want to make sure no names have been overlooked. However, if a client specifically wants us to mail the invitations, we would be happy to do so as part of an additional service.

What should the bride or groom-to-be include inside of their wedding invitations?

Apart from the obvious information such as the date, time, venue and RSVP, depending on the kind of wedding you are having, you may want to include the following as appropriate: a dress code, whether children are allowed or is it an adult only wedding; are you accepting gifts - if so, do you have a gift list, wedding registry or are you taking gifts in cash? It is important to include as much information as necessary to take the guess work out and make it easy for both you and your guests. Information useful to your guests such as a map or directions, accommodation available nearby, and a request for any dietary requirements or restrictions your invitees may have should also be included. This attention towards your guests and their comfort will make them feel their needs have been carefully considered, and they will appreciate the gesture. Music and songs are often played at Asian weddings. To make the invitation a unique and personal reflection of you as a couple, why not include a list of those songs and music meaningful to you both that will be played at the wedding or ask your guests to write down which songs they would like played.

Who should the response card envelope be addressed to?

The response card envelope should be addressed to whoever has been designated as the person who will collate all the responses and any follow ups as needed. This can be the couple, the parents of the couple, a wedding planner or someone else. The parents of the bride may want to be responsible for those invitees from the bride's side and vice versa. This is a very important role and whoever takes on that role, it is vital that they are organised, efficient and can respond to any questions from the guests as well as convey all information received to the appropriate person/people. Where necessary, they should send reminders to those who do not respond by the RSVP date.

What should a couple be careful of when selecting a wedding invitation designer?

Your wedding invitation is the first glimpse of the tone and quality of your wedding. It should stand out and be a statement of you as a couple. You need to make sure the designer understands you and the style you want; are they able to incorporate elements meaningful to you in the invitations? Do they have enough flexibility in their approach and designs so as to reflect you, your style and preferences? Your stationery designer must provide references and testimonials from previous clients. They should have a portfolio of designs to show you the quality of their finished work. Your wedding invitation designer must be detail oriented and be able to make sure even the smallest detail has not been overlooked. There must be uniformity across all stationery to give it a sense of cohesion and harmony like the theme, typeface and cardstock.

Does the stationery designer offer a seamless service which encompasses everything from designing to printing? This is a very important consideration. Your stationer's aim should be to relieve you of any stress, manage the printing process, provide a proof copy of the invite and offer advice. Make sure the stationer is able to create the look that's right for you. There are many choices available today to create the WOW factor without it costing you an arm and a leg, e.g. with creative use of fonts, colours, textures and cardstock. If you are having a multicultural wedding, has the designer any experience in that specialty? Hiring a quality designer with experience in multicultural weddings allows you to have those aspects, themes and symbols of your different cultures that are meaningful to you imaginatively woven into the entire suite of stationery. This makes a real impact and is a tribute to your individual heritages. An experienced wedding invitation designer will know the importance of small but crucial details such as including a map, directions, fact sheet, accommodation details, food preferences, etc. that give the invitation an overall look of professionalism. They should be able to guide and advise you on all those details so your invitees feel special and look forward to the event.

What are some of the advantages of hiring a professional wedding invitation designer as opposed to a couple creating their own invitations?

What couples planning a wedding should realise is that the cost of stationery is a much smaller component of the overall wedding budget compared to the cost of the venue, wedding dress, bridesmaids dresses, flowers, cake, etc. so there should be no need to compromise on the quality of the stationery. A professionally designed wedding card will be a unique statement of you as a couple and will incorporate those elements meaningful to you. A professional wedding invitation designer will provide high quality stationery whilst offering a personable and bespoke service to suit your needs, and keep within your budget. Professional stationery designers will ensure there is uniformity across all stationery to give it a sense of cohesion and harmony like the theme, typeface and cardstock. Professional designers are able to offer you a seamless service which encompasses everything from designing to printing, freeing up your time to focus on the other important preparations for the wedding. Bespoke wedding stationery means no one wedding invitation will be the same as the next, providing you with pure exclusivity. While creating your own wedding invitations will give you a sense of satisfaction, an important factor to consider is the amount of time involved. With your checklist sure to be getting longer rather than shorter as the wedding date approaches, having a firm control on time lines is of the essence when planning the wedding. You may discover too late that producing your own cards has set you back, especially when there are other equally important things clamoring for attention. If making your own cards, you may find it difficult to keep your invitations consistent in design or you may discover that by the time you have bought and put all the components together, financially you are no better off than having them designed professionally. So before you decide to get your hands messy, it would be wise to think about the amount of precious time, effort and energy needed to devote to creating your own stationery. Their expertise and experience will help you avoid many pitfalls and unforeseen challenges. After all, you want to be relaxed and energised on your wedding day!

Should the names of deceased parents be included on a wedding invitation?

Asian families generally want to mention the names of deceased parents in the invitations both as a way of including them on the wedding day and as a sign of respect. Some people mention the name/s of the deceased parent/s at the bottom of the invitation e.g. "With compliments of the late Mr/Mrs (name of the deceased)". If the bride is issuing the invitation and one of the groom's parents is deceased, then the invitation can say "son of the late Mr. (name of deceased)", and vice versa. Times are changing and there are no hard and fast rules unless you come from a very traditional family.

When a couple are paying for most or all of the wedding is it proper to put the parents names on the wedding invitations? If so, how should the parents be listed?

Asian couples do generally want to show respect towards their parents regardless of whether the couple is paying for all or part of the wedding cost. They are becoming creative about wording their invitations. One way to do it would be to say "Together with their parents...." or "Together with their families..." or again, they may want to mention at the bottom or somewhere on the invitation "With compliments of (parents' names)".

If wedding invitations are being sent to people who live at the same address, should one invitation be sent to each person or should one invitation be sent for everyone living at that location?

If it is a family living together and you want to invite everyone, the general rule is to send a separate invitation to the parents and also to every member of the family who has reached adulthood (generally 18 years). Children under the age of 18 can be included in the parents' invitation. Similarly, if a married couple is living in the same house, they should be sent their own invitation.

What are the options for colour, paper type, ink and fonts if a couple choose a custom wedding card?

A custom made wedding card will offer endless choices. The professional invitation designer will be able to show you a very wide range of options and you will definitely get the right look and feel of the card. In terms of the cardstock, some of the choices include metallic, translucent, handmade, silk paper, cards of different weights and colour. As far as the colour range goes, again there is an enormous choice. The designer will help you choose from metallic inks and regular inks, whether you want one colour or full colour, and what the final effect will be, together with the cost of each choice. They will also be able to show you the differences between screen printing and offset printing. In terms of which fonts to choose, it is the role of the designer to help you make the right choice. There are literally thousands of fonts to choose from but there are some fonts that are more appropriate for a wedding invitation. They need to be clear and easy to read, and if it is a colour font there must be enough of a contrast from the colour of the card itself, so the font doesn't merge into the background or people have to strain to read the words. The designer can show examples of various styles from their portfolio of previous work so you can get a real sense of how the various choices would look.

What other wedding stationary can card printers provide?

Other wedding stationery can include save the date cards, a welcome pack, place cards, monograms, order of service, menu, thank you cards, seating plan, table numbers, stickers/envelope seals, an information sheet to include maps, accommodation information as well as inserts of other functions such as sangeet, mehndi, and pooja, just to name a few.

HOW TO CONTACT US

Ananya : without equal – Orders and Enquiries:

Website: www.ananyacards.com

Email: info@ananyacards.com

Telephone: +44 (0)20 7242 1877

Twitter: www.twitter.com/ananyacards

Facebook: www.facebook.com/ananyacards

6.
HIRING A LIVE BAND - YOUR PERFECT WEDDING ENTERTAINMENT

Eastern Illusion are UK's premier innovative Bespoke Live Asian Music and Corporate Events Management Company for all occasions and various types of events, presenting high calibre; Artists, Professional Live Singers, Live Band, Asian Musician, Models/Hostesses, Specialist Acts, and much more! Setting a standard within the industry using a truly unique and personal approach in our work, Eastern Illusion is now recognised as being one of the top Asian events and management company within the UK and internationally. We are a group of professional, talented, energetic and passionate individuals and combined together carry over 15 years of hands on experience. We take pride in providing unique LIVE Entertainment and Services to all our valued customers. We as professionals are always looking forward to better our service, never resting on past accomplishments. Our goal is to treat each customer as an individual, each celebration as a one of a kind and to make your/any special occasion a classy and cherished memory.

What should a couple consider when choosing a live band for an Asian wedding?

We believe that quality should be your main concern when booking a band for your function. Choose entertainment that not only you like, but what suits the atmosphere of your wedding as well. Consider the taste of your guests, their age range and whether they would like to dance, listen to the music or a mixture of the two. If your family are appreciative of live music and enjoy watching performances, then there is nothing more romantic, classy, or exciting than live music at a wedding.

With live bands, does a couple have the ability to request specific songs? If so, how far in advance should the couple notify the band of specific song requests?

Yes, however most bands have suitable fixed sets/playlist that work well at weddings that they would like to go with and then add on the specific requests. Requests should be provided as early as possible to allow the band to prepare well in advance.

Do live bands generally take breaks throughout the event? If so, how many breaks are customary and how long do the breaks typically last?

Eastern Illusion Live Band configures their performance according to the schedule and specific requirements of your event. Each event is treated as unique and bespoke; this allows us to ensure that everything runs perfectly in accordance with your individual preferences. When the band is not playing or taking a break, we will always play soft background music or provide pre recorded background music through our sound system to insure a continuous flow of music.

What is the typical price range for a live band?

Prices vary between bands depending on size, popularity, singers profiles and/or other services included. Asian 7 Piece Live Band would start from around £1200.

What are some factors that generally determine the cost of hiring a live band?

Before you start researching various ideas, you may need to question the balance between costs vs. quality. However, do not risk the success of your wedding by opting with only the cheaper suppliers as many of them lack the necessary experience and reliability of professional wedding entertainers.

What are some things that a couple should consider when deciding which band to hire?

You might consider asking the following questions:

- How will the band dress?
- How long will each set be and how long will each break be?
- Will they be able to provide continuous music or taped music during the breaks?
- Will the band take requests?
- Are there any extra costs not included in the quoted fee?
- What is the payment schedule and cancellation policy?
- What is the hourly fee? Overtime fee?
- How long has the band been together?
- How long has the band been playing weddings?
- Will the band act as the Master of Ceremonies?
- If the band does not know a specific song that I want, will they learn it?

- Will the same musicians or DJ that I have seen or heard definitely be the one performing at my wedding?
- Does the band have Public Liability Insurance?
- Will the band need feeding?

How far in advance should a couple book a specific date with a live band?

Popular bands are often booked more than a year in advance, so the earlier you start, the more you will have to choose from. You should really start looking around 12 months before your wedding, especially if your wedding events are held on popular weekend dates. If you find a band that you like, find out as soon as you can if they are available. As soon as you make your decision, make the leap. If they aren't available on your date, at least you'll have plenty of time to find another.

What is the customary deposit that a couple normally places with the band?

Eastern Illusion Live Band requires 50% deposit to secure the date of the booking.

If an event needs to be re-scheduled or is cancelled, what is the latest that a couple should notify the band, in order to get their deposit back?

Every suppliers Terms & Conditions vary. Eastern Illusion cancellation and refund T&C's are effective from the date contracts are signed up to 30 days before the event date.

Are there ways to see or hear a band's music before making a decision? If so, what are some ways for a

couple to check out a band prior to making a decision to hire them?

Eastern Illusion provides samples of their music and videos of performances on the website, and this is a great way to see them and hear what we sound like. We invite potential clients to any of our live performances at any public events so they can be sure our band performance is suitable as well as check out the sound.

Can a couple usually decide how large the band will be?

As Eastern Illusion specialises in bespoke live entertainment, we allow our customers to choose the number of musicians/singers in the band to suit their tastes and budget. Firstly a couple would need to check that there is enough space for the band - It's no good booking a 10 piece band only to find that the performance area is 2 x 2 metres! As a general rule 5 x 4 metres is enough space for a band of 4 – 6 members, but the larger the line-up more may be required. For our customers who are contemplating on whether to have a live band or DJ, we also offer a lot of alternatives to suit individual requirements, such as a live singer performing to backing tracks with our DJ, or live background musicians as an added extra.

What are some other factors that should go into a couple's decision about hiring a band for their Asian wedding?

Firstly, you would need to check that your venue will actually allow you to have a band! It is a necessity to find out if they have adequate licenses and check that they have no obstructive noise or decibel limiters. In case there are noise restrictions, you can overcome this by perhaps booking a DJ or a 'quieter' style act (i.e. a Jazz band as opposed to a 'party' band).

Read the entire contract – from beginning to end! Along with the agreed price, the contract should state the date, starting and ending time of the event. It should also include the times for setup and sound check, as well as a clause stating that the act will perform at a reasonable volume as determined by a specified representative of the wedding.

Recommendations are always the best so pay careful attention to the entertainment at friends' weddings. Ask around to see if anyone has heard of a good wedding band lately and get references from people who may have booked them in the past. Thorough research is important to ensure that you are dealing with a reputable company. Professional suppliers should also be able to provide you with a list of venues or previous clients that recommend their services.

HOW TO CONTACT US

Eastern Illusion Bookings and Enquiries:
Website: www.easternillusion.com
Email: info@easternillusion.com
Telephone: +44 (0)20 8387 1951
Mobile: +44 (0)7958 734 311

7.
THE FIRST DANCE -
GETTING IT RIGHT ON YOUR BIG DAY

Honeys Dance Academy - Excellence in Bollywood Dance Training and Entertainment. Launched in September 1997 as the first British Asian Bollywood Dance school, Honey's Dance Academy (HDA) boasts an exciting range of courses ranging from fashionable Bollywood to upbeat Bhangra right through to traditional Indian Classical. The academy is proud to provide opportunities to students of all cultural backgrounds, abilities and ages, by involving them in entertainment related projects ranging from taking part in Bollywood films and dancing in pop videos right through to participating in student stage shows. HDA offers the highest level of training with classes run by teachers of the highest calibre who are considered the best in the country. The academy allows students to take accredited Bollywood dance exams and offers training to beginner's right through to professional instructors. Apart from specializing in offering Dance training, HDA also provides Bollywood Dancers and Choreography services to stage spectacular dance entertainment at weddings. HDA wedding entertainment packages can also feature a collection of interactive services to make the Bollywood entertainment experience more memorable – From fun dance Workshops staged at Mehndi nights, amazing dance routines taught to friends and relatives to perform at family weddings, providing social dance training to enable any beginner to perform basic dance steps at parties, right through to step by step dance training offered to wedding couples to transform them into graceful performers for their special first dance.. No matter if it is a major headliner for a fundraiser, a dynamic party for a corporate extravaganza or a black-tie gala right through to co-ordinating artists for a Bollywood film set, Honeys Dance Academy promises something for everybody.

Honeys Dance Academy was founded by Honey Kalaria, a Bollywood dancer, choreographer and actress, who has been involved in Bombay Dreams, Merchants of Bollywood and Bride and Prejudice, with TV appearances on Bollywood Star, Ruby Wax, This Morning, Top of the Pops, Blue Peter, Jamie Oliver and MTV's Bust a Move. She has worked alongside Gareth Gates, Beyonce, Craig David, Shah Rukh Khan, Hrithik Roshan and Aishwarya Rai. Honey broke the Guinness Book of World Records on Sky TV by getting the largest number of studio audience to learn bollywood dance in the shortest time. Honey has worked as a choreographer for Gurinder Chada's latest film "It's a wonderful afterlife" and appeared as a choreographer and trainer to professional performers on BBC's "So You Think You Can Dance". Together with Honey Kalaria, a team of dedicated staff members run Honeys Dance Academy, each sharing a vision of changing people's lives positively through Bollywood Performing Arts.

What should an engaged couple bring to their dance lessons?

For a first dance training session, the couple should bring along a Music CD with a selection of their favourite songs, bottle of water, comfortable clothing, a camera to film the routine learnt in the class as a memory jogger when practicing back home. It is also important and advisable for the instructor to see the clothing & shoes in advance (especially the brides) to ensure that the couple can perform their routine and move with ease whilst wearing the wedding outfit.

Why should an engaged couple take dance lessons prior to their wedding?

There are many reasons for couples to take dance lessons prior to their wedding. A wedding is a very special occasion and most of the times, a once in a lifetime event, so worth investing some time in ensuring great memories are captured on film for the couple to share with others and watch many years later. A first dance is important to include in your wedding celebrations program as it allows the couple to have centre stage on their special day, and be able to display their love and togetherness by a beautifully choreographed couple dance routine and of course by taking the lessons in advance the couple can perform in a seamless and co-ordinated manner which is sure to impress the audience and guests attending. An added benefit is that whilst learning dance, the couple can spend quality time and have some fun together whilst the busy wedding preparations are going on.

Should the engaged couple already have their wedding song picked out, prior to their lessons?

It does not really matter! If the couple is not sure then the professional instructors can discuss with the couple, and help them choose an appropriate popular slow song from a compilation that has been prepared in advance. Alternatively, the couple may bring along a few favourite songs to choose from, which they would enjoy performing their first dance to. We normally find that it is important to choose a song which the couple can relate to and has a deeper meaning for them. The song lyrics and music can be selected depending on the message the couple wishes to convey to each other, as well as communicate what they mean to each other to others.

How long should the couple's main wedding dance?

2 - 3 minutes of a beautifully choreographed and co-ordinated first dance is enough to create a powerful impact, and allow the audience to give the couple 100% of their attention. After which the family and audience members should be encouraged to come onto the floor by the DJ or band to join them. This would also be a great way to start the party and dancing for the special occasion.

What are some of the most popular Asian dance styles for a couple's main wedding dance?

The most popular styles are mainly a slow Bollywood love song with great lyrics and music that the couple can dance to (although we have had couples requesting a first dance to be performed to an English song). The routine can be made of various moves depending on song, music and theme such as bollywood combined with salsa turns, ballroom patterns across the dance floor or Latin American steps added to bollywood or even bhangra steps. Important thing with the routine is that it should look intimate, close and display good interaction between the couple.

How many lessons should an engaged couple typically take, so that they are prepared for the big day, and what will they learn at these lessons?

We normally recommend anything between 2-6 hours, but the time depends on how fast the couple pick up the dance steps, how much dance training or skills each individual has and how advanced and complicated the couple would like their routine to be. 12 hours of training would enable the instructor to choreograph a breath taking dance, even if the couple are complete beginners who have never danced.

Do the bride and groom both need to attend the dance lessons at the same time? If not, how do dance instructors typically work around situations where both people can't be present for their lessons at the same time?

We would definitely recommend both partners to attend together as the routine is couple based, it is important that both people get used to performing with each other. This could include how the couple hold hands, how the male should be holding the bride, the posture both need to display, how to develop looking comfortable dancing with each other, learning how to show facial expressions and interacting with each other whilst dancing to ensure that they perform seamlessly and with ease during their first dance. This also allows the instructor to choreograph the routine according to the level of both partners, as one may be a stronger dancer then the other. If for any reason both can't attend together then it would be advisable for them to attend together for the first dance lesson where the trainer will ascertain their requirements, level of skills and choreograph a routine for them accordingly. Both partners will then be taught the routine separately and then invited to come for their final dance lesson together if possible. If not then a filmed copy of the routine with steps broken down can be provided to each party to practice in their own time at home after each lesson. Another great advantage of learning together is that the couple can also spend quality time together, have fun and enjoy the wedding journey and each moment along the way.

What are some of the main differences between group and private lessons? What are the advantages and disadvantages to each?

Main difference is that you get personal attention and individually tailored dance routines based on your requirements and dancing level when learning one to one in a private lesson:

Advantages and disadvantages of Private lessons:

1. Song and style of dance can be personally selected by individual

2. Instructor can give personal attention and focus purely on the individual(s) taking the class

3. Instructor may be able to dedicate more time to offer invaluable advice on how to build up the strengths and improve specific weaknesses of the individual

4. The choreography set for the dance routine would be individually tailored to help achieve specific goals

5. The individual may be trained at their own pace, taking into account their capability and skills

6.   Private lessons are more costly

Advantages and disadvantages of Group classes:

1.   You can come along with friends, have fun and meet new like minded people

2.   In a group, an individual starts learning faster by watching others and having to keep up

3.   The space can be used creatively by use of patterns and floor spacing with larger groups.

4.   It is more cost effective paying for a class in a group

5.   You may feel shy and not very confident if you are a total beginner and put in a large group

6.   It may get frustrating for those wishing to move faster but have to move at a slower pace, to enable the instructor to cater for all levels of dance students

Should the couple wear any specific types of shoes to their lessons?

We would advise all students to wear comfortable shoes whilst learning dance such as trainers, jazz shoes or even bare feet. If the training is for a first dance at a wedding, then it is highly advisable to practice one or two lessons in the shoes you will be wearing during your wedding to get used to the shoes which for the bride is normally high heels.

What is the best way for a couple to select a wedding dance studio and/or an instructor?

Ensure that the academy / dance instructors have credibility, experience, good testimonials, they are friendly and a good level of service is being provided. It is important for the academy and instructors to be able to understand your needs and requirements. Try to book a studio with mirrors as this is very important. This will enable the couple to learn much faster as they will be able to see themselves dancing and try to rectify any mistakes being seen.

Does the couple typically bring their own music to each lesson?

Once the music has been selected it is useful for the dance student to keep a copy of the music CD in their bag and bring it along each time you attend the classes. Normally, once music is selected and agreed, a professional instructor will keep the music CD copy with them and bring it along to each lesson.

What if the bride-to-be or the groom-to-be is far more experienced in dance than their partner? Is it still possible (and advisable) to take lessons together?

Yes definitely, we truly believe that the couple should come together – the dance classes are not just about the end result, but also about the journey! The classes will give the couple a chance to spend more time together, learn a new skill together, have fun together, bring the couple closer and learn dance steps that they will be able to use at many parties in the future as a couple. The more experienced partner can be encouraged to support their partner during dance training and when they go back home to practice.

What types of clothing should the couple wear to their dance lessons?

The kind of clothing that the couple should wear during their dance training is anything comfortable and not too restrictive. Keep fit wear is fine. Depending on the choreography and song selected, sometimes women are advised to wear a skirt to help her feel more feminine and allow the hip movements to be seen more clearly. We would also recommend that the couple should do a dress rehearsal where possible, and practise their routine in their wedding outfits that they will be wearing. Sometimes we find that the bride and bridegroom wishes to keep the outfits as surprises – on this occasion we would advise them to bring similar outfits to practice in.

Is a wedding dance usually a choreographed pre-planned routine?

Wedding dance choreography is normally individually tailored for each couple, depending on the song selected and their level of skills. A few pre planned routines of different levels are also available that can be taught if the couple are unsure of what song or theme to select.

How far in advance should a couple start taking dance lessons before the big day?

HDA believes that it is better to take the dance lessons in advance. In this way there is no panic, unnecessary stress and if any changes need to be made, or more time to practise needs to be invested then there is time! After learning the routine, the couple are invited to book a refresher lesson anytime between a few days or a few weeks before their big day. It is good if the couple are ready 4 weeks before their special wedding day. Having said that, we have taught couples a dance routine on the week or a few days before their wedding by offering an intensive 6 hours training session in one day, and the couple have looked stunning during their big day.

HOW TO CONTACT US

Honeys Dance Academy Bookings & Enquiries:
Website: www.honeysdanceacademy.com *or*
www.honeykalaria.com
Email: info@honeysdanceacademy.com
Telephone: +44 (0)78 5087 5087
Facebook: www.facebook.com/officialhoneykalaria
Twitter: twitter.com/#!/honeykalaria
Linkedin: www.uk.linkedin.com/pub/honey-kalaria/a/14a/834

8.
GETTING INTO THE GROOVE –
HIRING THE RIGHT WEDDING DJ

Sensation Entertainments has been going for 10 years and we are a DJ company based in the North West. We are a small friendly team, who work closely with brides and grooms to organise the perfect entertainment for their wedding without breaking the bank. We are professional, experienced, and flexible and do our utmost to give our clients a personalised and excellent event that won't be forgotten. We have a huge collection of music ranging from Bhangra, Bollywood, RnB, English Pop, Motown, Disco and even work with styles such as Salsa!

How far in advance should a couple book their DJ?

We always recommend the earlier the better, from experience a lot of people are organised and will book early, sometimes a year in advance, but typically most couples usually book about 6 months in advance. Usually during peak seasons, we always advise couples to book early to avoid being disappointed if their desired DJ is unavailable for their wedding date. In addition, by booking early you have the peace of mind of knowing that you have one less thing to book! It's not uncommon for people to call us a few days before their wedding to book! By leaving things to the last minute, couples would have a limited choice of which DJ companies are available.

Are all DJs required to have insurance? What type of insurance should couples check to make sure their DJs have?

It is not essential, however, a lot of major venues now expect DJs to have public liability insurance and as such most DJ companies now have their own public liability insurance – it is always a good idea to ensure that the DJ has a minimum of £2 million over. Wedding co-ordinators at your venue would normally advise you if insurance is required and often documents can be sent to the venue in advance to confirm that insurance is in place. It is also recommended that even if the venue does not require insurance, that you use a DJ that is insured as it gives you that peace of mind that they do take health & safety matters seriously and there is protection in place in case of any accidents.

How far in advance of the event should the DJ arrive at the event?

This is very much dependent on the set-up that is required – usually for a smaller set-up, 1 hour in advance is normal but for larger set-ups we recommend 2 – 3 hours is allowed for setting up. Therefore, set-up time needs to be factored in putting together a schedule. It is worth also bearing in mind that if a ceremony is happening in the same room and a DJ is not required until later on, that there should be an opportunity for the DJ company to come in and set-up either right at the beginning of the day or if there is a suitable interval during the event.

Are there any setup or breakdown fees that the couple is required to pay?

There should not be any additional setup or breakdown fees required when booking a DJ but always a good idea to check what the cost of a package covers.

Can couples typically request specific songs they'd like the DJ to play? If the answer to this is yes, how and when should these requests be made by the couple?

Yes, absolutely and couple can request songs for their wedding! Most good DJs have a huge collection of tracks old and new from a wide range of genres. Some couples prefer to provide a full list of the songs that they want on the day whereas others choose a handful of songs that carry some kind of meaning and let us choose the rest of the music. We are happy to work either way and normally ask for song requests to be provided by email at least a week before the event.

Do Disc Jockeys usually play requests made by the guests? If yes, how is this typically done?

A good DJ will be willing to accept requests from guests on the day itself and encourage people to come up to the DJ box to make a request. We offer a unique service where guests that are coming to a particular wedding can log onto our website and request their favourite songs in advance to avoid disappointment. In the rare chance that we do not have a particular track requested on the day, there is an option to try and download the track using mobile Internet – the joys of modern day technology!

Can couples request specific songs that they don't want played at their wedding? If yes, how is this handled?

That is absolutely fine; couples can have a list for the DJ of songs or genres of music not to play on the day. In the same manner that a request list is taken, an additional list of 'do not play' songs can be produced too. By offering this information it is really useful for the DJ to ensure that music provided is as personalised as it can be to your wedding.

What are some extra services that a couple can add on to their wedding packages?

This is dependent on the DJ Company but typically most can offer screens for couples to display family photos, dhol players (Punjabi drummers) for entrances, dance groups and confetti cannons to name just a few extras! If you want any extras, it is always a good idea to ask at the initial enquiry stage as there is a good possibility that you could get a good rate if you booked a number of services together.

How can a couple see a DJ "in action" at an event, prior to deciding whether or not to hire them?

It is usually possible for a couple to see a DJ in action; however, arranging a meeting is very much dependent on agreeing with the other couple who are getting married. For most people, this should not be a problem to arrange. If it is not possible to arrange this, many DJs have their own video clips on YouTube to give couples an idea of how they work and the type of events they have done previously.

What if the DJs equipment breaks during the wedding?

DJ companies such as ourselves always carry back-up equipment but when booking couples should check their individual DJ company's policy on break downs, as this can differ from one company to the next.

How does it work with deposits? Specifically, how much should a couple place down for a deposit and when is the balance due?

In order to secure a particular date normally a 50% deposit is required which can be paid by cash, cheque or via secure online payment. Couples should always get a receipt for all payments and the remaining balance is usually paid on the day itself at the start of the event. Although only a deposit is required, some couples prefer to pay the full amount in advance, which is another option for couples who do not want the worry of making payments on the day.

If the event needs to be cancelled or re-scheduled, when is the latest that the couple should notify the DJ?

As soon as a couple are aware that an event needs to be cancelled or re-scheduled then the DJ should be notified as soon as possible. Sometimes it can be difficult for a DJ to accommodate a re-schedule but most DJs will try to be as flexible as possible but this can be tricky during peak wedding season. When an event is booked, usually the DJ would keep that date free, hence turning down other weddings, so if there is a cancellation, it would it is likely that if you have paid a deposit that you could lose the deposit paid. It is always recommended that before booking any wedding service that you are 100% of the date to avoid any problems later on, although there maybe circumstances beyond your control, we always encourage couples to speak to the DJ as soon as possible if there is a problem.

What should a couple pay attention to when interviewing DJs for their big day?

Sometimes it can be easy to just focus on who is the cheapest, however, it is important for couples to bear in mind, what are the DJs communications skills like? Are they friendly and approachable? How willing are they to play that music that you want? Do they have testimonials from satisfied customers? Do they have insurance in place? How much experience have they got?

HOW TO CONTACT US

Sensation Entertainments Bookings and Enquiries:
Website: www.sensationentertainments.co.uk
Email: contact@sensationentertainments.co.uk
Telephone: +44 (0)7936808447
Facebook : www.facebook.com/sensationent

9.
HENNA - ADDING THE MAGIC TOUCH
TO YOUR BIG DAY

Mehndi Creations offers you a unique, new generation henna art and design service, combining elegance and sophistication, adding the magic touches for that very special occasion. Whatever your style or taste from Arabic, traditional Indian, Mogul to more Contemporary, modern designs, a touch of glitter and coloured stones can be used to accentuate the hues of the chosen outfit. Mehndi Creations have successfully showcased work for various Corporate events (Cartier, Proctor & Gamble, Dubai Tourism, HSBC), Virtual wedding shows, Bafta goes Bollywood Event, In-flight Magazine (Serendip), Asian wedding magazines, Asian wedding fairs, Miss Movie pageant shows and celebrities like Karen David, Konnie Huq, Kara Revel, Sanjay & Pooja Shah from Eastenders, Sam Sterling (Popo Gigi), and Raghav. The main artiste Khilna, offers a highly personalised, friendly and tailor made service to suit individual tastes & budgets. She specializes in Bridal Henna.

What should a bride look for when selecting a bridal henna artist?

There are several factors the bride needs to consider when choosing the appropriate henna artist.

- Experience – understand the clients' requirements

- Versatile and creative - be able to recreate traditional and modern designs.

- Quality of Work i.e. type of henna used, colour, depth of stain but especially the design and styles. Apart from this, the henna artist should also provide post henna application measures, so that the Henna stain is very dark and it lasts for a long time.

- Provide Consultation & Trials – During a consultation, the artist should also be able to understand the bride's requirements and show ideas of what can be done. The design can also be selected by keeping the bride's dress in mind and the embroidery on it as some of the shapes can be infused into the design. It would be good if the artist offered a trial to get an experience of what the style and colour of the henna stain would be like. The stain of the Henna is the dominant feature whereby most brides now prefer to have the darkest possible colour.

- Ability to travel – there may be a call out charge or depending on the package the bride booked it could included.

- Understand budgets – there are 100's if not 1000's of henna artists in the U.K. all with individual pricing, however as this would be the only time the bride get the opportunity to get a bridal Mehndi, she must consider that experience, quality of work and colour comes at a price.

- Insurance - be aware that the artist has public liability insurance

- Portfolio and website - The Artist must have a website and a portfolio of work for the clients to see. Henna artists should offer a wide-ranging variety of designs as-well as henna bridal packages suiting the client's needs.

- Specialist in henna - Avoid paying the all in one price i.e. hair/makeup and henna all done by the same person, since the person may not be specialising in any one field.

What are the different types of henna styles that exist?

Choosing a nice henna style and design will make the bride's hands look very beautiful. The henna designs are always changing each year. Recently, a lot of my clients have requested the full, intricate, traditional henna incorporating the wedding/shaadi figurative story. I would design a story on both hands and feet which comprises of the grooms arrival to the wedding venue and the brides in her doli. Apart from the modern designs used as tattoos and body art, there are many distinguishable designs for henna as shown below. To beautify the henna for henna nights, wedding or receptions, body glitter and gems in different colours can be applied on the skin to match the outfits.

The designs I create, are a mixture of freestyle shapes, symbols, lines, etc, originally from ancient art from different countries. There is a huge variety design categories which include:

Arabic Henna Designs – large flowing patterns, incorporating paisleys, swirls and flowers. Usually animal motifs, bird motifs and human faces are not used due to the religious reasons.

Traditional Indian Henna Designs – intricate designs with fine lines, leaves, peacocks, paisleys, flowers, lace, auspicious and religious symbols. Figure-work incorporating the bride and groom's faces may also be used. These designs usually cover the entire hands and feet.

Contemporary or Traditional Henna Designs – Similar to the traditional Indian designs but more spaced out with a contemporary touch to it.

Indo Mogul Designs – A combination of Indian and Mogul Arabic patterns with smaller shapes.

North African Henna Designs – Large but intricate designs with peacocks, butterflies, flowers, fish, geometrical shapes.

Celtic Designs, Chinese symbols, Religious symbols, Animal art and tribal art designs are also created for henna tattoos which can be applied for both men and women.

Is it common for henna artists to have a portfolio of their work?

I strongly recommend that the brides should see the artist's portfolio beforehand to see what the artist can do and offer. Some artists only show their magazine work, however a portfolio is essential to get a better idea of the artist's work. I would also initially look for the artist's website, which would bring confidence and show previous work for the bride to select before the consultation.

Do henna artists offer to do small sample designs at bridal consultations?

Most henna artists offer small sample designs/trial at the bridal consultations. For a bride, it's very important to have a sample design to get a feel of the style and colour of the henna stain, as there is no point having the best design and after get a light or dull colour. Sometimes, brides have already seen the stain on their friend/family's Henna but it's still better to have a small sample done. However, remember there may be a charge for this facility.

How should a bride prepare for a henna session?
I recommend that brides should have manicures, pedicures & waxing done before the henna session. A bride should also avoid applying moisturizers or oil on the skin before hand as this will affect the absorbency of the henna paste.

What colour will natural henna stain?

The henna powder can be a khaki, green or dark brown colour depending on where it comes from. It usually develops into a reddish, chocolate, brown colour when applied as a paste onto the skin. Fresh henna paste will produce a strong dark brown colour and will last longer, whereas stale henna will produce a light orange colour, which will not get darker over time. The use of black "henna" should be avoided as it contains a dangerous chemical called Para-phenylenediamine (PPD) found in hair dyes which causes skin irritations.

What if a bride has her own design? Can henna artists work with custom henna designs?

A professionally skilled and creative henna artist will be able to adapt to the bride's requirements and therefore, if a bride has her own design, the artist should be able to work with this as a reference or customise the design to create something unique.

Generally do henna artists charge by the hour, per hand or per job?

Various henna artists charge in different ways. Some charge by the hour, while others charge by the number of hand designs done. Most Bridal Designs are tailored into Bridal Packages and priced accordingly to make it easier for the bride and also to offer an incentive to book the most suitable package.

Do brides have to provide their own henna paste or do henna artists bring their own?

Henna artists usually bring their own henna paste in cones as they are used to the flow and consistency of the paste. It is also better this way, as the colour of the stain is more likely to be good if the artist is reputable.

What are some of the basic safety precautions when applying henna onto the skin?

It is advisable to use natural henna paste and not the black henna on the skin. By using henna paste in its most pure form, you will highly reduce the risk of irritation on the skin.

How long does it normally take to apply bridal henna?

It can take anything from a couple of hours to a few hours depending on the intricacy of the henna design and how high up the arms the bride wants it done.

If a bride has a certain colour palette in mind for her wedding what are some of the ways a henna artists can incorporate this into the henna art?

Body glitters which come in various shades and colours can be used to match the colours of the brides colour palette into the henna art. These glitters can be applied with crystal gems to highlight the henna, however this is only temporary and will normally last a day.

Can henna artists apply henna to other members of a wedding party at discounted rates?

Other family members are usually done at a discounted hourly rate if booked with a bridal package.

What is the best way to care for Bridal henna after it has been applied?

There are many ways to care for the henna post application:
Once the henna has been applied on the skin, it may be left overnight or left on for at-least 4 hours to enhance the deepness in colour. It is best if the hands are not washed on the same day as application. The henna can be scraped of with a payment card or the blunt side of a butter knife. The henna on the skin should not be covered with a plastic bag or gloves as it will result in condensation from sweating and therefore loose the definition in design. Lemon Juice & sugar syrup can be applied with cotton wool on to the henna once it is dried. This will secure the henna paste onto the skin. The colour on the skin will darken on the day after the henna has been applied. The darkness in colour will last for a few days and will fade away. The warmer you are, the darker the henna colour comes out on the skin. The old wives tale goes "The darker the colour the more your husband loves you!" Excessive washing and lotions may also affect the colour of the henna stain.

HOW TO CONTACT US

Khilna Shah, Mehndi Creations Bookings & Enquiries:

Website: www.mehndicreations.com

Email: info@mehndicreations.com

Telephone: +44 (0)7944004299

10.
STYLISH TO THE SOPHISTICATED -
CREATING YOUR PERFECT
WEDDING DRESS

Based in London, **Inspiration Couture** brings a collection of authentic and modern ready-made outfits from bridal to casual wear, along with exquisite Bollywood inspired outfits custom made to measure and designed by renowned Delhi based designer Sagun. Our readymade collections range from designer suits, bridal outfits, party wear, casual and menswear. So whatever the occasion, Inspiration Couture has an outfit for every individual requirement. If it's a Bollywood outfit that inspires you, like Katrina's black sari worn in Singh is King (Teri Ore) or the pink lengha worn by Deepika Padukone in Om Shanti Om (Ajab Si), Inspiration Couture can take this or any other design and ingeniously tailor it so that it's unique to you. Having worn many of Sagun's designer creations, made with alluring fabrics and enchanting creations, Anshu launched Inspiration Couture with Sagun. Together they are determined to use their expertise and eye for detail to not only create exquisite outfits inspired by Bollywood, but also provide a host of captivating readymade outfits.

As a leading actress in the South Indian film industry, Anshu has appeared in many movies alongside actors such as South Indian superstar Nagarjuna, Prashanth (famous for movie "Jeans" with Aishwarya Rai) and Bollywood actress Sonali Bendre. With a national Filmfare award for the best female newcomer in the film Manmandudu, Anshu has also been brand ambassador for many high profile brands in India including Indian Airlines, Francis Alukkas Enterprise and Colgate. For your bollywood inspired outfit, just email a photo or web link of the outfit that has captured your imagination, and we'll create a unique custom made design as per your needs. If you prefer a readymade outfit, we have an extensive collection of beautiful designs for any occasion. We aim to bring quality, exceptional service and affordability to our clients. So go ahead, indulge yourself, whether it's a readymade design you love or you're inspired by the latest Bollywood trend, look no further – Inspiration Couture – be inspired.

What information should a bride gather before she starts her search for the perfect wedding outfit?

Brides must ensure they have an idea of their dream wedding outfit. This could be something they have always had in mind. It may even be something inspired from a Bollywood film which is always the majority of the case. Brides should ensure they have all the vital facts about styles, budget and even feedback from fellow married women on how they found their search for that perfect Wedding outfit.

What questions should a bride ask a dress designer or boutique to help her determine which boutique or dress designer she should trust and buy from?

Prospective brides should be able to ask EVERYTHING & ANYTHING from a dress designer/boutique. This is the most important day of their life and possibly one big investment too. Questions can vary from designs, styles, fittings and price (bargaining). If the designer is happily able to answer all questions openly and run through all the facts then they are right the designers to go for. It is always worth checking with others their thoughts on the particular brand as well as homework via numerous search engines or prior customers.

What are the different types of outfits typically available in Asian Bridal Wear?

The list is endless! A bride can go for a Royal Lehenga, to a bridal saree or even a mesmerising Punjabi Anarkali suit. Asian Bridal wear is huge! The latest trend has become typical gowns with an eastern fusion too.

What sort of things should a bride consider when deciding on which type of wedding outfit to choose?

Brides must consider a number of things. These can vary from choice of colour, the heaviness of the attire (considering they will be wearing it all day), at times there may be a dress change so possibly not. Budget also plays a huge factor as well as style and embroidery work.

How much time should a bride allow for her initial appointment to discuss her perfect wedding dress?

A bride should typically have a 2 hour consultation with the designer/boutique to determine exactly what she is after and how this can be implemented.

What type of dress silhouettes suit which body type?

The quality in Asian Bridal wear is that the traditional saree can suit all body types- whether you are tall or short. The traditional saree gives the bride a very slender and toned look. The traditional lehenga on the other hand would not be perfect for all body types. The latest trend again to give the slender and toned look would be the fish tail style lehenga skirts. These are the best form of outfits for the slim and average body types whilst going for a more straight cut skirt for the curvier bride.

How does the process work for ordering wedding outfit and having it ready in time for the big day, from initial order to first fitting?

All designer/boutiques must cater for all types of future brides and treat them all as individuals which they obviously are. Spending years, months or even days could seem a stretch for some, whereas for others a typical requirement. Some prefer to see what they like via an online store and purchase exactly that sending across their measurements so it can be custom made to measure. Others prefer a consultation, feel of fabric and fitting. A range of services must be offered! It is highly suggested that brides go for a consultation so designers can figure out what they have in mind or even help them with ideas and styles. The fabric and outfit is purchased and tailored to their specification. For custom made designs our production team spend between 4-12 weeks creating the perfect wedding outfit with every intricate detail.

Why would a bride custom order a wedding outfit as compared to purchasing one that is already in the store?

Some boutiques may not have what a bride is after, so why would a bride want to limit their choices? A good Bridal boutique should be able to create whatever a bride wishes, whether it's an outfit inspired by the latest Bollywood trend or one created by an in house specialist.

What is the average price range for a bridal gown and what determines this price range?

For a ready to wear bridal gown brought by us prices can vary between £100- £1500. This is all dependent on the fabric and stone work. The more work the higher the price. Custom made designs can be in the same price bracket and more. Again this is all dependent on what the bride is looking for.

What is the customary deposit needed for ordering a wedding outfit?

At Inspiration Couture we take 50% deposit and the remainder on completion. This should be the same in most boutiques/online stores and by designers.

Why would a bride need to order extra fabric and why is this sometimes requested?

This is always requested by brides in case they decide to have extra sleeves, coverage/alterations or simply in case of weight fluctuation before the big day.

What is a "hollow-to-hem" measurement?

This is a difficult measurement to take and taken from the base of the neck just above the collarbone to the hem. Whilst taking this measurement the tape must be taken away from the body to determine the fullness of the skirt.

What should a bride bring to the alteration fitting?

When a bride goes for an alteration fitting it is best to come in comfortable clothing, and bring the shoes that will be worn on the day.

Should a bride call in advance, to schedule an appointment, if they are coming in for a fitting?

Yes, we highly recommend this. This will ensure the designer is completely dedicated to the bride for her special day.

How soon before the actual wedding day do you recommend a final fitting for a wedding outfit and why?

We generally recommend 2 weeks before the wedding day for a final fitting. This is the perfect time frame should there be a likelihood of the body shape changing. We do discuss exercise and diet with our clients to assess when the final fitting should be. If exercise is vigorous then we ensure that the final fitting is a week in advance.

What is the best way for brides to store their wedding gown before and after the wedding?

We supply appropriate packaging where the dress can be stored simply without causing any damage to the fabric and dress itself.

What are some of the common things that can go wrong when custom ordering a wedding gown and what should a bride look out for to ensure smooth process with as little stress as possible?

Common things that can go wrong in production are if extensive changes have been made from the original consultation. If a brides constantly changes, adds or takes away designs from the attire this can cause a lot of issues or likelihood of mishaps in production. This is why having a consultation is imperative. Everything should be cleared within a 10 days of placing an order. The best way to ensure a smooth process is for a bride to avoid making too many changes after an order has been placed and for the designer or boutique to ensure they keep the bride updated with the progress. It is always nice to reassure the bride.

HOW TO CONTACT US

Inspiration Couture Orders and Enquiries:
Website: www.inspiration-couture.com
Email: info@inspiration-couture.com
Facebook : www.facebook.com/inspiration.couture
Twitter: www.twitter.com/#!/InspirationC

11.
LOOKING RADIANT ON YOUR BIG DAY –
FINDING THE RIGHT MAKE-UP ARTIST

Karismha Hair & Makeup is based in Wembley Middlesex London, specialising in English, Indian and Asian bridal hair and makeup and special occasion party hair and makeup, bridal makeup. Karismha is a freelance Hair & Makeup Artist and a qualified and experienced holistic therapist, providing services in London & surroundings areas. Karismha Hair & Makeup has been featured in the Asian Bride Magazine in the Makeup Artist portfolio. Karismha Hair & Makeup has also featured in the Asiana magazine.

Karismha Hair & Makeup creates an individual look for each bride, be it glamorous, traditional, modern or a timeless classic look that radiates the brides own beauty & captures the hearts of all guests. Bridal trials are advised to discuss bridal requirements and advice and looks that flatter the bride are suggested. Karismha offers beauty treatments, makeup lessons, and indulgence and pampering parties ideal for birthdays, children's parties, weddings, anniversaries or girly get-togethers. Karismha also specialises in corporate wellbeing with pampering days available.

What should a bride look for when selecting a bridal makeup artist?

The first thing you should look for is the professionalism of the makeup artist, are they organised when you arrive, their behaviour and attitude towards you as a person and others they are talking to, their etiquettes, their approach to their work is it casual and carefree attitude or is it professional but friendly? - if the makeup artist doesn't have passion towards their work or has bad manners it will eventually come out on the client or show in their work. Look at their work, their website, and their reviews as a makeup artist. Are they hygienic when working? This can usually be seen during a bridal trial. What type of makeup brands do they use? Also ask friends who have got married as word of mouth is always useful. Is the makeup artist flexible do you feel comfortable with her as you will have to start your big day with her? Does she listen to what you want or is she doing something totally different to want you want? Does she advise you on certain looks?

Some makeup artists can take on more work and can tend to give less time to the individual on the day. Ask the makeup artist if they have other bridal appointments after them, especially if you have booked the makeup artist for the morning registry and then for your Ceremony or reception later – the last thing you want is for them to rush off in between and then they arrive too late for your services in the afternoon or evening.

Does the entire bridal party normally use the services of the makeup artist too?

Usually the entire Bridal Party requires hair and makeup services and can be booked through the makeup artist as they have a team of hair stylists and makeup artists to work on your bridal party whilst the main makeup artist works her magic on the bride. It is always best to ask if your makeup artist's team is available on the same date as they can be sent out elsewhere. If makeup artist team is unavailable you know immediately so you can start searching for another team to take care of the bridal parties requirements separately.

How long does the whole process take?

The Entire time scale for an Asian Bridal look can take 4 /5 hours from beginning to completion, depending on complexity of hairstyle chosen whether a hair extension is required, the complete bridal makeup, assistance with dressing which includes draping of the Dupputa or sari dressing and Jewellery Assistance. Asian Bridal Makeup is no small job it requires complete focus and attention to detail. Complete bridal makeup can include up to 5 or 6 shades of eye shadow in different textures and colours that require blending, false eyelashes, liquid eyeliner on top and kaajal, it can be dramatic to subtle yet still the attention and intricacy of work requires upmost attention, it can also include Bindi " Peer " decoration that can be hand painted by the makeup artist in a various designs on the forehead or nowadays decorative stick on Bindi's are in fashion and are more popularly used.

Is it best for the bride to have her hair done first, before the makeup, or the other way around? Please explain why it's best for one to be done before the other.

The bridal hair style should be done first so the makeup looks fresh when the bride appears in front of her guests. If the bridal makeup is done during hot seasons especially in spring and summer the makeup will tend to melt away and fade if done first and will need to be retouched after doing the hair and causing more work for the makeup artist and taking up more time in the long run.

How do makeup artists work with clients who have sensitive skin and various skin types?

A detailed one to one Consultation with clients is required this is one of the reasons why a Bridal Consultation is required first to find our if the client has sensitive skin, what skin type the client has and what products she is currently using. A professional make-up artists will also find out if the client is doing a proper cleansing routine, if the client has any allergies to certain skincare, makeup products or brands so that they can be totally AVOIDED for that client. All these allergies must be noted in a clients file and followed by the makeup artist. Some clients can suffer from nut allergy in oils and creams, lipsticks or even false eyelashes this is all discussed in detail at the consultation so that precautions are taken and suitable products are used for that particular client.

It is always important for all brides to have facials a couple of weeks leading to the wedding day so that any skincare issues can be dealt with. In a facial a detailed skin analysis is given to find out the client's skin type under a magnifying lamp, to see if there are any blemishes, uneven skin tone, blackheads, pigmentation, fine line and wrinkles or spots. On the basis of the skin analysis the correct products are prescribed to the client to suit their skin conditions. Certain Products such as " Fragrance Free " Products, skincare products free from chemicals "parabens" are also advised to be used for sensitive skin types this will calm any aggravated skin. It is essential that the client follows a daily regular skincare routine leading up to the wedding. If the client has oily congested and acne prone skin and even the most expensive makeup was used it can still make the appearance and hard work of the whole makeover look awful. The clients face is like a "blank canvas" to the makeup artist and the makeup is the art work of the makeup artist, like a painting. However if the canvas, the "facial skin" looks uneven, spotty with large open pores the effect is not so appealing. If the skin is smooth and flawless the makeup will glide on effortlessly giving a balanced look and a great end result which is more appealing to the eye.

Will makeup typically be used that has been used on other clients? What sanitary factors should a bride ask about when speaking with a makeup artists?

Makeup artists can use various methods of precaution to prevent cross contamination of makeup; firstly separating desired makeup into a makeup palette can prevent the same makeup being used on different clients, the main ones to look out for are powders, foundations, lipsticks and eye pencils. The bride can ask what sanitary precautions are used when using makeup on clients, she can also observe when having her trial if the makeup artist takes out a fresh pair of brushes for the trial that is a good sign! If the brushes look dirty and used it is a sign of a carefree attitude, ask the makeup artist to use fresh ones or steer clear of that makeup artist as that could spread infection. The use of wet wipes during a trial indicates the use of hygiene. You can always ask if the eyeliners and lip pencils have been sharpened, a professional makeup artist will always sharpen and clean their makeup kit after using it on a client, so it is neat and clean for the next client. Always see if the makeup artist washes her hands or uses a hand sanitizer before and after your makeup session!

What is airbrush makeup?

Airbrush Makeup is a spray on method of applying makeup similar to airbrush body tanning a special hand held spray gun is used with the certain colour required which is are poured into the gun, together the colour with the air pressure the airbrush makeup can be applied. Airbrush makeup requires skill and precision which should be applied by a professional makeup artist whom specialises in airbrush make up. In Airbrush make up the foundation can be applied to get a darker sun kissed look, blusher eye shadows to lips can be airbrushed. This is used widely in magazines, photo shoots and film, the most popular airbrush makeup is the foundation to get an even tanned look for brides.

Is it a good idea for a bride to wear lashes on her special day if she's not used to them? Why or why not?

At a bridal trial it is essential for makeup artists to ask the bride if she has worn false eyelashes before, if she is ok to wear them, or if she has extremely sensitive eyes. These questions will inform the makeup artist whether to use false eyelashes or not. Wearing false eyelashes especially for Asian brides certainly gives the WOW factor as they enhance the eyes and draw attention to the most prominent feature on the face, adding a touch of glamour to the whole look and giving the eyes more definition in the wedding photographs.

Most brides do not have any problems wearing false eyelashes; however it is always important to test them at the trial to prevent any hiccups on the wedding day. Usually false eyelashes only feel uncomfortable for a few minutes then the bride gets used to them and forgets about them. However the makeup artist must ensure that the false eyelashes selected for the bride match the brides face shape and eye length as overly exaggerated heavy false eyelashes can ruin the look too. If you know you have sensitive watery eyes just inform your makeup artist to stay clear of them, as watery eyes will prevent the glue on the lashes from sticking to the eye lid.

What are the best types of makeup products for a bride to wear on the big day?

- Waterproof Lengthening Mascara in Black or Brown depending on client skin tone, the best ones are YSL, Lancome or Christian Dior
- Mac Photographic Foundation that will last throughout the day.
- MAC Pigment Eye shadows that have prominent colours that will stand out and stay all day. This comes in different shades.
- Staywear Lipstick by Estee Lauder or Lipstick in applied layers with the option of lipgloss on top instead of just lipgloss as it will not last.
- A hydrating oil free moisturiser

How does a makeup artist ensure that the bride looks good on her big day, both in person, and in photos too?

- A Bridal Trial will first ensure the bride is happy with the look of what she desired as any changes can be made on the bridal trial to ensure the bride is happy. If the bride is not happy at the trial she will not be happy on the day, the trick is to ensure the makeup artist works to get the look the bride is happy with, once the bride is happy with the end result this increases self confidence in the bride which will show in the wedding photos. All the products used to achieve the look on the trial should be recorded and pictures taken so that the makeup artist knows exactly what makeup should be done on that particular bride and for what function. If the make-up artists is organised this will make the bride feel at ease knowing that the makeup artist is organised and this will automatically make the bride feel relaxed and happy which will show in her photographs.

- The makeup artist should study the clients face shape so that the client's best features can be accentuated and highlighted such as cheek bones, eyes and the nose. Certain areas on the face can be concealed using shaders to contour and define such as the bone structure, such as a large nose can be made to look narrower, cheeks bones can be defined, areas can also be shaded so that less attention goes to those areas, this is done by facial contouring techniques by using highlighting and shading techniques, making the bride look defined in the photographs and in person.

- A makeup artist must ensure the bride is following a regular daily cleansing routine at home using the correct products for her skin type as the wrong use of skincare products can lead to more skin problems along with professional facial treatments to treat and balance any skin issues prior to the big day.

- A good makeup artist will advise the bride of do's and don'ts such as make sure the bride gets a good night's sleep before the wedding this will prevent dark circles or puffiness under the eyes.

- Relaxation techniques such as deep breathing to help calm the bride are advised, as well as hot baths to soak the muscles and induce relaxation

- If the Makeup artist is a professional and qualified beauty and holistic therapist a "Holistic Approach" can be offered to the bride as planning a wedding whether on a small or on large scale has the same amount of pressure and anxiety resulting in mental and emotional stress and muscular tension, which in turn leads to physical exhaustion. This is why natural holistic therapies are advised to relax the bride. The most popular treatments such as the Famous Chakra Hot Stone Full Body Massage, Swedish or Aromatherapy massages using essential oils, Ayurveda massages such as hot poultice all massages can help to eliminate toxins, improve blood circulation and ease muscular tension which will help the client to relax on a mind body and soul level leaving her revitalised and rejuvenated for her big day. Pamper parties for the bridal party are a popular day for all to interact and relax before the big day.

- To help the bride relax and to be calm on her wedding day and talk to her as a friend but also being a professional at the same time, a balance is key. Finally remind the bride to just enjoy her wedding day and smile as day has finally arrived which she has been tirelessly working towards for months.

- The makeup artist also gives tips to the bride to help her keep her makeup looking fresh throughout the day, such as how to remove sweat without removing makeup, how to keep lipstick from getting on the teeth, how and when to top up lipstick during the day, what brushes to use and keep on her and also to have a reliable friend on hand who she can rely on to make sure she is intact throughout the day after the makeup artist has left.

What factors and options usually determine how much a makeup artist charges?

This can depend on the level of experience, skill, professionalism, expertise, where the makeup artist has trained, at what academies, their qualifications, any famous celebrities they have worked on, the products and brands they use, who they have worked with, the area they work from, the level of service they provide and most of all what exactly the brides wants if it is a full bridal service including makeup hair and dressing, travelling or just one particular service, also the style of makeup and hair they selected as hair extensions are an extra however the bride has the option to have the hairstyle she desired instead of waiting for her hair to grow.

Do most makeup artists do pre-wedding consultations with the bride and the wedding party? If so, what is typically discussed at a consultation?

It is essential to have a detailed Pre bridal Consultation to help guide the makeup artist to help achieve look the bride has in mind if they have one. The makeup artist can also suggest looks that will flatter the bride, things the makeup artist will take into consideration is the age, the skin tone, the outfit being worn, the texture of the hair, the skin, any allergies to products, any cut outs from magazines of particular looks, the hair length, what hairstyle will suit the client, to go half up half down to the side or keep the up, what the client will feel comfortable with, is the bride changing her hair colour will she be wearing contact lenses etc, the colours the brides like and what she doesn't like is also discussed.

How far in advance should a bride book a makeup artist?

Ideally the consultation can be done 4 to 5 months in advance to ensure the wedding date is available, as of peak season dates get booked early especially in the summer months. If the bride is 100% sure of the date and wants a particular makeup artist you can also book a year in advance depending on how each makeup artist works.

Does the makeup artist typically come to the bride, or does the bride travel to the makeup artist?

Most Makeup artists travel to the bride's residence or venue to provide a stress free service to the bride and the bridal party. A makeup artist usually covers the surrounding areas, some travel, nationwide and some internationally, with their equipment and staff.

Does the bride usually need to have special equipment such as special chairs, lighting, or mirrors for the makeup artist?

A professional makeup artist usually carries a lot of equipment to provide a good service to the client; this can include a high makeup artist's chair so the makeup artist can work at eye level without straining her back for long periods of time and prevents straining the client's neck. Lighting that is used in hotels to give maximum light to see the work being done, most makeup artists also provide hair services so a professional hair kit is always carried, containing various brushes, hair products, heated rollers, heated hair tongs and hair extensions in different shades. Usually the makeup artist would already have separated the exact makeup that is required to achieve the look that was done at the bridal trial, saving precious time on the day. However as a standby, a professional makeup artist will always be prepared and carries their makeup and hair kit as standby just in case there are any last minute changes or any extra people to cater for. The kit should include various eye shadows, lipsticks, foundations, skincare, eyeliners disposables, clean makeup brushes; they never travel without their full kit to always be prepared.

What are the main differences in make-up style for a traditional Asian bride and modern bride?

A Traditional Asian Bride will want:

- A Bindi "Peer" decoration hand painted by the makeup artist on the forehead

- Traditional heavy and rich makeup colours of Red and Gold must be used on the eyes, together with other colours in the outfit to compliment the outfit can be used.

- Red / maroon lipstick

- A "Tikka" an important Bridal Jewellery ornament applied to the brides forehead

- A Heavy Sari or 2 in some cultures must be worn for a traditional wedding ceremony or a heavy Indian wedding attire called the "Lengha".

- In some cultures heavy eyeliner is required and a lot of definition on the accentuation on the eyes is demanded by certain brides

A Modern Asian Bride would require:

- Less makeup is a popular request is "NOT a caked look", not too much foundation as some brides ask to go few shades lighter to look fairer on their wedding day

- A more natural look and not too heavy look

- Accentuation on the eyes but paler lips

- More natural tones such as peach, bronze

- Pastel colours to be used instead of traditional red and gold colours

- Modern stick on bindi's only around the eyes or in between the eyebrows instead of all around the eyes

- More and more brides are now opting for different colours for the wedding day rather that the traditional red so other eye makeup colours can be used such as pinks, purple, greens, blues and oranges.

- A more glowy fresh dewy complexion, rather than heavy an matte
- Liquid foundation with minerals for sparkle for a more natural look

---

HOW TO CONTACT US

Vandana Malhotra - Karismha Hair & Makeup Bookings and Enquiries:

Website: www.karismha.co.uk

Email: info@karismha.co.uk

Telephone: +44 (0)7952 122 411

Facebook : www.facebook.com/pages/Karismha-Hair-Makeup/135795086531539

12.
PROFESSIONAL OR CONTEMPORARY - HIRING THE RIGHT PHOTOGRAPHER FOR YOUR WEDDING

I am the owner of **Tapas Maiti Photography**. I specialise in photography for Hindu, Sikh and Mixed Faith weddings and my goal has always been to provide artistic documentary photography with a mix of fashion and beauty thrown in. I always photograph every wedding since my approach is based on building a strong relationship with my clients from the initial meeting through the wedding and beyond. I do the photography, editing and album design so that you get a set of images that are bespoke and reflective of my style and my knowledge of you.

What are the advantages of hiring a professional wedding photographer as opposed to having a friend or family member take the pictures?

Many amateurs can be great photographers but with a professional what you really get is peace of mind and hopefully an assurance that your wedding photos will be special. A professional wedding photographer will have a lot of experience of delivering greats photos consistently and in all conditions. It is easy to produce a portfolio with 15 great photographs but a professional needs to deliver consistently great photography no matter what. A good professional photographer will take the time to know you and draw on that knowledge to deliver something special. On a more mundane note though, you need to remember that a professional will have back up equipment, a network of colleagues to provide support in an emergency and insurance should something go wrong - all this does cost them money but its part of being a professional. My final word on the matter however is quite simple. You will have invested a lot time and love into your wedding day and in the years to come your photographs will hold those memories, nothing else will with quite the same power.

Why do wedding photographers copyright the pictures they take at weddings? Is this common?

It is important to understand what copyright is; it is the ownership of the image and the ability to control it and make money from it. What is important for a customer is to be able to use their wedding images and I provide my images, properly edited in high resolution with the rights for almost unrestricted personal use: copy them, put them on Facebook, make prints, give them to friends and so on. I offer this with every package and for every client.

Is it better to book a wedding photographer who uses film or digital equipment?

Book a wedding photographer on two thing alone - do you like their work and will you get on with them personally. You don't ask a plumber what wrenches they use or a surgeon what brand of knife ? I use film for some of my personal work and digital for my professional work and whilst I have a real soft spot for film , I will generally use what is most appropriate. Digital technology enables shots in the most atrocious lighting conditions and it also allows for a larger number of images to be delivered at a wedding. Film is more of an artist's medium - its gives the most amazing colours for skin and has a natural organic feel but it is more expensive and you would need to understand the restrictions; fewer images per wedding, the need for better lighting as well as the costs. If I had a free hand and was shooting a wedding outdoors, I might want to use film, in a dark venue in winter, it would have to be digital.

What is a proof and what are the advantages of the different types of proofing?

A proof is just a quick edit of your wedding images for you to look at and choose. Before digital, a photographer might get the film processed and get very cheap machine prints done as these are much cheaper. These would be given to the client and from their selection a set of final prints done at a pro-lab. Options also exist for making a book of proof. Nowadays most proofs are done digitally and given on CD or via an on-line gallery. Personally, I don't see the point, I select your images and edit them and then provide them on a gallery for you to see and then you get them all high-res and looking beautiful.

What are the pros and cons of hiring two wedding photographers to take pictures at a wedding, as compared to only having one photographer taking pictures?

Two wedding photographers allows you to work different parts of the venue, capture different angles and themes. For instance one photographer might follow the bride, and the other the groom. This can be very useful for certain types of wedding such as Sikh Weddings where the groom will have morning ceremonies at the same time as the bride is getting ready. One disadvantage is cost, you either pay a lot more or you get "cheaper" photographers, the other disadvantage is of course that the more photographers and videographers at the wedding the more intrusive it becomes. I have been to weddings where there might have been two photographers and 3 videographers for me it was awful. I prefer to work solo or with an assistant because I want to capture the wedding, not change or control it.

What types of wedding packages do photographers typically offer?

The range of options is huge but generally speaking you will get maybe 3 or 4 options which you can build one , these will offer different hours of work and different albums or CD only packages. Generally most clients want coverage for a certain number of hours and an album and you don't want to force them to buy stuff that they don't need so extras will generally be options on top.

What is the customary deposit to put down, to reserve a photographer for a date?   When is the balance typically due?

Again this varies considerably; I require a £300 deposit with the balance paid 2 months in advance, some photographers will require a large deposit but will allow you to pay much closer to the date. I would suggest that deposits of greater than £500 are too high unless you are getting some sort of discount.

Why is there such a large price range among different wedding photographers?

Two reasons really, the first is the cost base of the photographer and second factor is their quality. Someone shooting on a cheap camera with no back up and working a full time job can afford to price for next to nothing but if you want a photographer that uses good quality equipment, pays insurance and invest time in their skills, you need a full time or part time professional ; they then need to make a living out of it. Unfortunately the digital revolution has made everyone think they can take good pictures but this is just not true. The quality factor is also important - when photography reaches the quality of art, it is no longer a generic product; not everyone can draw like Van Gogh and the best photographers have an eye an imagination that cannot be replicated. The best wedding photographers in the world are artists; they do not trade as companies and will offer you a really unique vision.

At what point in the wedding planning process should a couple book a wedding photographer?

Once you have a date and venue, its a good time to start the search but of course this depends on your priorities and how important the photography is to you. Just don't expect to get a really good photographer with a month to go unless you are really lucky.

What should a couple look for in a wedding photographer?

Most importantly, you need someone you get on with, special photos need a good rapport and your photographer will be with you all day. After that you need to pick a photographer whose vision and style matches what you want; if you want hundreds of posed photos don't pick and 'artistic' or 'documentary style'; if you want natural, emotional images then don't go for a 'traditional photographer'.

What should a couple beware of with certain wedding photographers?

Most professional are trying to do the best job they can, just be sure that their work suits what you need and price matches what you are getting, there is no such thing as a free lunch so if a deal is too good to be true... The key things though are to be sure that you know who will do the photography at your event and meet them personally. Don't invest time in a company and then find you don't know the person turning up.

How should a couple determine their wedding photography budget?

This all depends on how much money you have available and how important photography is to you. There is always a trade off between quality, time and budget and many good photographers may offer you a deal if you can compromise on other areas e.g. the number of events or the number of hours you need.

What equipment should a wedding photographer have?

This will vary on each photographer's style and approach. I carry very little equipment but what I have is of the highest quality because I want to be fast, flexible and unobtrusive. More important to this is a photographers approach to back up. I have lights, spare cameras, and spare lenses available in my car or in a separate bag just in case something breaks, I may never use them but I invest thousands in back up to minimise the risk to your big day.

What happens if it rains?

A professional photographer needs to produce the results whatever the weather conditions; I carry beautiful white umbrellas in my car just in case. My cameras are water resistant and I can always find covered areas to get nice shots.

Do prices typically vary for off-season or weekday weddings?

Asian weddings tend to be year round but you may get a discount for additional ceremonies which are quite important for Asian weddings or if you are a personnel recommendation but it also depends on how much demand there is for your preferred photographer.

What other important points should a couple consider before hiring a wedding photographer?

Consider the costs for everything you need, I make sure that my clients know the prices of all their potential options in writing and guarantee those prices on booking the wedding. Also consider whether you are getting a photographer and videographer whose styles will match. You will need to choose what is more important to you and work from there.

HOW TO CONTACT US

Tapas Maiti Photography Bookings and Enquiries:

Website: www.tapasmaiti.com

Email: enquries@tapasmaiti.com

Telephone: +44 (0)1223 244855

13.
UNIQUE, ELEGANT AND AFFORDABLE – CHOOSING THE RIGHT BRIDAL JEWELLER

PureJewels is a fine jewellery brand established for 36 years and has been recently voted amongst the top 50 most inspiring independents in the UK by Retail Jeweller Magazine. PureJewels has been celebrated in the UK for its heritage and support of emerging jewellery design talent through their Platinum Heritage Project which invites designers to design a couture piece of platinum jewellery, taking inspiration from the brand's cultural journey, the journey from India to England via East Africa. PureJewels is also the headline sponsor for the UK's most established 'PureJewels presents Asian Wedding Exhibition' that takes place every year at Alexandra Palace and is currently running in its 19th year.

What should someone look out for when selecting a jeweller? Specifically, how can they be sure that they are getting what they're paying for?

To be appointed as the jeweller to make your engagement and wedding ring is a great privilege for any jeweller and it is important that they are passionate about their business and what they do. You will find with any business, whether it is a hairdresser, dress maker, cake maker or cabinet maker, if the company you deal with are passionate about what they do then you will get great results because they will go the extra mile for you. As a general rule, I have found that businesses that focus on their product and customer relationship are generally very successful. Also, fine jewellery is required by law to have a hallmark which guarantees the quality of the metal and also diamonds generally come with an independent certificate of authenticity and quality.

What are the "four C's" with regard to diamonds and what do they mean?

The "four C's" of diamond quality was developed by the Gemmological Institute of America (GIA) and defines the diamond's authenticity and quality. This grading standard has been adopted by jewellery professionals around the globe.

The **colour** hues of diamonds range from being colourless (D colour) to being light yellow or brown (Z). Most diamonds used in jewellery are nearly colourless and truly colourless diamonds are very rare therefore much more expensive.

Diamonds are formed under tremendous heat and pressure and therefore will exhibit some internal and external characteristics that are a by-product of their formation. It is extremely rare to find a perfectly clear diamond and the **clarity** of a diamond is graded as being either flawless (FL), very very slightly (VVS) included, very slightly included (VS), slightly included (SI) or included (I). A stone that has some internal characteristics is a quick way of identifying a natural diamond to a synthetic one.

The **cut** refers to the quality of the cutting of a natural diamond and is measured as excellent, very good, fair or poor. The beauty of a polished diamond lies in its complex relationship with light, how light strikes the surface and how much light enters the diamond and what form of light returns to your eye. Brightness, fire and scintillation are three attributes that describe this light. The brightness refers to the white light reflecting from the surface and the interior of the diamond. The fire describes the 'flares' of colour emitted from a diamond. Finally, the scintillation describes the flashes of light you see when the diamond, the light or the observer moves.

The **carat** weight is the measure of weight of a diamond where one carat is equivalent to 200 milligrams in weight. Similar to currency, a diamond is divided into 100 points.

The combined measure of the "four C's" provide a way to objectively compare and evaluate diamonds and this helps to price diamonds more fairly. Ultimately, your chosen jeweller will have an eye for a beautiful diamond and can advise you on the best balance of quality, beauty and price.

What is an "Ideal Cut"?

Polished diamonds that are graded as "excellent" in their fine proportions, symmetry and polish to optimise their interaction with light are considered to be "ideal cut" stones. The result will be to have a stone that has increased brightness, fire and scintillation. In fact, ideal cut diamonds will reflect nearly all the light that enters it.

What is the difference between a "certified diamond" and a "non-certified diamond"?

There are a number of independent gemmological laboratories around the world, the most recognised are the Gemmological Institute of America (GIA) and International Gemmological Institute (IGI) for certifying diamonds that weigh above a quarter of a carat. There are also independent gemmological laboratories that specialise in certifying diamond studded jewellery like Solitaire Gemmological Laboratories (SGL) for small diamonds already studded in jewellery. A certificate gives you the reassurance of authenticity and quality and gives you the peace of mind that you are getting good value for money. It also allows the jeweller to be associated with such trusted institutions and shows good practice.

Generally, goods which are certified are more expensive than non-certified diamonds, but this is because of the additional cost of securely sending items to such laboratories, the administration and the cost of the service and the time it takes for the items to be returned back into stock.

What is a "ring setting"?

The ring setting is normally referred to as the prongs or claws that hold the diamond in position. There are many styles of setting available which are defined by the shape of the stone. A four prong setting on a round diamond very often makes the stone appear square so many women go for six prongs for a round diamond. The only downside to having a six prong is that the stone is not as visible as it would be in a four prong. Many designers are often given the challenge of using the least possible number of prongs while still ensuring the stone is securely set. For small diamonds, it is always worth asking the jeweller what warranties they have if a small diamond falls out from its setting. Another thing to remember is to consider how a ring will look over time when hand cream residue accumulates, it is very useful to ask if the jeweller has a lifetime valet service to ensure the diamonds and the ring setting is maintained and checked regularly. Classic ring settings will be about showing off the centre diamond to its full magnificence. It is also quite trendy to enhance this with having small diamonds set in the shoulders and creating different types of looks.

Whatever is chosen, it is important to ask yourself if you will still love the design after ten or twenty years.

How does a man determine the ring size of his future fiancé, if he wants it to be a surprise?

The tradition of buying a ring and proposing is always the most romantic way to propose. In modern times, women appreciate it if the ring buying experience is done together as a couple. It is a great experience to take your fiancé ring shopping and getting her to choose the setting of the ring. To avoid any embarrassment, the most expensive part of the ring is always going to be the centre diamond, so purchasing the diamond beforehand and proposing with the diamond will be a great way of asking and then going ring shopping. To set the diamond and choose a unique ring setting will add to the whole shopping experience and ensure that the ring is made to measure and fits perfectly. If you want to be a traditionalist and must propose with the finished ring, then getting your future fiancé's friends to help will be a great way of getting an approximate size – they could discretely get her to wear one of their rings to determine size. Another way would be to borrow a ring she wears on the right hand ring finger and take it to the jeweller to measure.

What are the common metals used when designing an engagement ring? How do these various metals impact the final price of the ring?

The two most considered metals for engagement rings are gold and platinum or a combination of the two. The most popular setting for diamonds is in platinum. Apart from its preciousness, the metallic properties of platinum make it a better performance with wear and tear over time. The feeling of luxury also comes from the metal being a little heavier than gold. A lot of women who like to have a combination of naturally white metal with yellow metal will decide to have the prongs to be made with platinum and the rest of the ring (the shank) to be in eighteen karat yellow gold.

White gold is an alloy of yellow gold and very often is rhodium plated to make it look as white and bright as platinum. I personally like the natural colour of white gold which is an earthy grey-brown colour and contrasts beautifully with diamonds. For a naturally white metal, platinum is the most elegant metal to use. Platinum may be a more expensive option, but in the context of the price of the diamond chosen, it may be worth to pay a little more and have the platinum option. Also, choosing platinum for the engagement ring also means that you have committed to the wedding ring to be in platinum as well. So it is always worth checking the extra price in platinum combined with the extra price of the equivalent platinum wedding ring too.

What are the common diamond cuts used in the design of diamond engagement rings? Do these various cuts impact the price? If so, how?

There is a great variety of diamond cuts available, the most popular and costly is the round brilliant cut diamond. There is a growing trend for women to wear unusual diamond cuts that are not popular because it makes their ring unique. Princess brilliant cut is a square shape and this influences the style of ring design. The basic shapes are round, square, rectangular, oval, triangle and eye shape. The square and rectangular shapes have the most variants in style of cut, for instance you can get square princess which is a 'brilliant cut' and has the most facets, square emerald which is a 'step cut' and has fewer facets but allows the light travel through the stone. The radiant cut, which was especially designed for fancy coloured diamonds is becoming more popular but is a deeper stone so doesn't look as big for its weight. The cushion shapes are a good way of combining round and square for a softer square look. The prices do vary according to cut and shape but not as much as the colour and clarity influence price, so it is really about personal preference.

What are some of the common diamond settings found in the design of an engagement ring? Does the type of setting impact the price?

The focus and purpose of a well-designed engagement ring is to show off the magnificence of the main diamond. Good designers will be sensitive to ensuring the diamonds look their best without compromising the safety of the stone. Good jewellery stores will carry designs that are considered and meaningful and reflect the romance of the occasion. Generally, rings will have additional diamonds or will be plain with two, four or six prongs of varying sizes. The price difference is very much directed by the extra diamonds used to enhance the look. The plain bands will all tend to be similar in price which will be influenced by their uniqueness, metal content and also consideration of design. It is also worth checking the luxury and comfort feel of the inside of the ring to ensure that you will enjoy wearing it all the time. Also, looking at the ring using a jewellers' loupe which magnifies it at ten times will allow you to appreciate the craftsmanship and attention to detail. Again, the very passionate jewellers will have already considered these aspects to make sure you get the very best quality and value for money.

How far in advance should the wedding bands be ordered?

The engagement ring purchase should always be done in consideration with how the wedding band will look with the ring, as this is the look she will be carrying for most of her life. For complicated designs it is always a good idea to order the wedding ring at the same time as the engagement ring to ensure that they are made perfectly together in one manufacturing process. A good jeweller who values the relationship they have with the couple will allow you to hold the wedding ring in reserve until you need it for the wedding for a small deposit. Generally, wedding rings made to measure to the finger size could take two to eight weeks to manufacture and plenty of additional time should be given just in case there is quality or size issues and need to be adjusted. An organised jeweller will constantly keep you updated with the ring progress and if there have been any delays.

How important is it for the bride's wedding band and engagement ring to match? What should be considered to ensure that the engagement ring and the wedding band look good together?

If an engagement ring and the diamond is the ultimate symbol of love then the wedding ring is the ultimate symbol of commitment. The idea that the two sit perfectly in unison is the most elegant design consideration for a couple. A good engagement and wedding ring design that follows a particular design narrative will already take into consideration the style of wedding ring hence the importance of always choosing or considering the wedding ring during the engagement ring purchase. If you want a greater choice of wedding rings and also consider how an eternity ring will look in the future then a diamond setting that is slightly higher will allow for the wedding ring to sit comfortably with the engagement ring. There is also another aspect to consider for the wedding ring that it looks great on its own without the engagement ring just in case the engagement ring has been taken off for cleaning or repairs.

How can an Asian bride determine what type of Bridal Jewellery will be right for her?

The wedding jewellery buying decision is very much driven by the wedding dress and the colours used. For exclusive precious metal jewellery women are more likely to choose a piece that is neutral in style so that the jewellery can be worn more often. A lot of brides are now opting to wear colour co-ordinated costume jewellery for the wedding day which consists of a large ornate necklaces, head pieces, large earrings, lots of bangles and hand pieces adorning the henna tattoos of the occasion.

Brides who are considering buying precious jewellery are more likely to buy exclusive design considered jewellery that they can enjoy on many occasions and not just the wedding, this has to be said for even the most exquisite diamond jewellery that may be worn during the civil ceremony and then can be worn to cocktail events. For brides, the wedding occasion is the best time to invest in beautiful individual pieces of statement precious jewellery that will get worn on occasions of future importance after the wedding, that way you know that the investment is worthwhile.

What are the different head pieces available that form part of an Asian Bridal set?

A bride can wear a number of head pieces for the Asian wedding ceremony and the most popular is the 'tika' which is a single line of adornment that covers the centre parting of the hair and the pendant section just covers the forehead above the centre of the eyebrows where a bride will also wear a 'bindi'. A much more ornate style of 'tika' head piece would be a 'bandi' with chains covering the hair line to just above the ear. This is extremely decorative and can also be worn with an additional head piece which is worn diagonally on one side of the hair called a 'passa'. Women are also adorning their hair plaits with jewellery ornaments that follow the full length to the waist. Asian jewellery is known to have an adornment for every art of the body and the wedding occasion is the time that brides enjoy dressing up in full glamour.

What other pieces of Jewellery can form part of an Asian Bridal Set?

The Asian wedding is known for bangles and every dress is colour co-ordinated with costume jewellery bangles intertwined with a couple of symbolic gold bangles for the occasion. The hand also gets adorned with a five ring bracelet that is called a 'poncha' and modern versions have a single ring style. A nose pin and earrings with a chain linking into the hair are all exciting elements of enhancing the beauty of the day. The look is as ostentatious as possible and colour is an important part of the day.

How important is it to order warranties and insurance for engagement rings, wedding bands and/or bridal sets?

Good jewellers have a well-established department for after sales care and general cleaning, checking of stones and repairing as an important part of the service. Additional insurance can be bought from you home insurance or specialist insurance companies for loss or accidental damage. A good jewellery company will be able to provide the service of giving you a valuation for insurance purposes. There may be a small charge for this service and needs to be updated every two years to take into account the constant fluctuation of gold, platinum and diamond prices.

HOW TO CONTACT US

Pure Jewels Orders and Enquiries:

Shop: 290 -292 Green Street, Forest Gate, London, E7 8LF

Website: www.purejewels.com

Telephone: +44 (0)20 8470 1221

Facebook : www.facebook.com/pureJewelscom

Twitter: www.twitter.com/#!/purejewelscom

14.
CAPTURING YOUR DAY IN STYLE WITH THE RIGHT VIDEOGRAPHER

JSV Media was founded by Jatinder Vaid. I became a Cinematographer after viewing my own wedding video, as well as those of friends and family, with great disappointment. This gave me the inspiration and motivation to become a Wedding Film Cinematographer. I believe that just because anyone can 'video' a wedding, that you should not choose just anyone. You should look for quality, passion and pedigree. I love my work and take great pride in the product I create for you. I aim to be as unobtrusive as I can on the day, allowing you and your guests to be as natural as possible. I recognise that there can sometimes be reservations about being filmed, but I, and my crew are often complimented on the day about our ability to work without causing undue distraction or attention. My aim is to raise the bar when it comes to filming weddings, opting for a more Cinematic look.

When selecting a wedding videographer, what should a couple take into consideration?

The most important thing in my opinion is the style of the videographer. As videography is a creative art, not all videographers have a set way of filming and editing, each has his/her own styles. Therefore, you should firstly view samples of their work to ensure that you will be happy with the end product. Secondly, ensure that you see an example of the end product, as sometimes the 'promotional' material can differ from what will be given to the client. Always meet up personally with the videographer as this is someone who will be capturing your special day for you to view for the rest of your lives. It is essential that you 'get-on' with the videographer and that you are all 100% sure as to what is needed in the end product. If you do not feel comfortable with the videographer then do not book him/her as you might regret it later. Obviously there is always the question of the budget, but ensure that you are not being charged for services and/or equipment that you do not need.

What are some of the options and features that a couple should consider for their wedding video?

Options vary according to videographers and budgets. Some you could consider are:

- DVD/Bluray or both
- Camera crane
- Steadicam
- Short-form and/or long-form edit versions
- Videography or Cinematography style of filming
- A pre-wedding music video shoot of the couple
- Guest messages
- MP4 version of video to be viewed on mobile, tablet computers.

How many cameras and camera operators typically film a wedding?

This really depends on the budget and scale of the wedding. Some couples can only afford a One camera shoot, whereas others have been known to book up to 5 cameras for a single wedding. Typically you should consider having a 2 camera shoot as this will allow your final product to have more of a 'film' look by capturing the action from different angles, as well as getting family & friend reactions. It also allows for 'redundancy', in that if 1 of the cameras fails during the shoot, you will at least have footage from 1 of the cameras.

What is the customary procedure for placing a deposit and paying the balance?

All companies differ in their operating procedures. However, be ready to pay at least a minimum of 10% upfront and at least 50% by the wedding date. I would not recommend paying the whole amount upfront. Once your end product is ready for delivery to you, then you should pay the total outstanding balance.

How do wedding videographers account for and handle various lighting conditions?

Lighting is always a problem at weddings, as the couple usually wish to have some kind of 'mood' or ambience within the venue. Therefore, it is essential that you inform the videographer as to what light conditions he/she can expect at the venue. This will allow the videographer to bring the right amount of light and place it accordingly. The traditional 'on-camera' light is still used to fill in faces during filming, however a professional will never use it to its full capacity as this is when guests will find him/her to be obtrusive and have reservations about filming.

Try to book a meeting with the videographer at the venue, this will allow both parties to get a better understanding of everything.

What type of equipment should a good wedding videographer use?

Wedding videography style has changed quite dramatically over the past couple of years as Cinematography has made a big impact, however the minimum equipment that every videographer should have are:

- Full 1080p HD cameras,
- Professional tripod, monopod equipment,
- Professional lighting,
- Professional audio capturing mics.

Depending on budgets you can also consider

- Glidetrack,
- Steadicam,
- Crane/Jib,
- Aerial photography capture equipment.

What is the standard attire/dress for the wedding videographers and can couples usually make special requests in this area?

The traditional attire has always been a suit and tie. However, you will find that most videographers who like capture the action from differing angles will not wear a suit as this can be very restrictive and make it difficult to work in. Therefore, decent comfortable work clothes is what is usually worn, and in black colour so as not to be too visible.

Is it customary to provide food for the videographers?

Food and drink should always be provided for the team of videographers. Consider have a table made up separately and ensure that you do not ask to have 'everything' filmed as usually the guests at the wedding will not like to be filmed whilst eating. This is an opportunity to give the videographer a break.

Is it typical for the wedding videographers to take breaks during the wedding? If so, how many breaks are standard and how long should each break typically last?

One break should be enough, and could last up to 30 minutes. This is usually taken when the food is served to the guests.

How long does it usually take, after the wedding, for the couple to receive their wedding video?

This is a question that you should put forward before booking the videographer. If a videographer says that he can get the end product to you in a couple of weeks then usually his work cannot be up to a very high standard, or he must be getting the video edited by someone else. The normal amount of time is anything between 1 to 3 months, and be sure to ask who will be doing the editing.

If a couple wants certain things excluded from their wedding video, how and when should this be communicated to the wedding videographer?

It is essential that this is communicated before the editing work is commenced, as once the final product has been made it will be costly to make amendments. The reason for this is that the video would have been edited to some kind of music, and if there are scenes that need to be re-edited then this can disrupt the flow of the rest of the film. Add to this the time it will take to render out the final film again, master the final DVD/Bluray, and also to burn the final DVD/Bluray.

What is same day edit and what other extras can videographers generally offer beyond the basic coverage of a wedding reception?

A same day edit is a short summary done at the end, or during the day, of footage shot. It is a very rough edit and is not something that most people would recommend, unless you are happy to have something to view just for the sake of it. Something else that could be offered is a guest message option where guests could leave messages for the couple to be viewed either at the end of the day, or put onto the DVD/Bluray as an extra. A Cinematic style trailer is something which can also be offered; this can be done within a week of the wedding and will allow footage captured to be viewed more professionally.

HOW TO CONTACT US

JSV Media Bookings and Enquiries:
Website: www.jsvmedia.co.uk
Email: enquiries@jsvmedia.co.uk
Telephone: +44 (0)1332416417
Mobile : +44 (0)7984669949

15.
PLANNING YOUR IDEAL DAY WITH THE HELP OF A TOASTMASTER

The London Toastmaster is a descriptive and definitive occupational title for Richard Birtchnell who is a Past President of the Society of London Toastmasters, the original and most prestigious professional Toastmasters' organisation in the UK

What is the difference between a Toastmaster and an MC?

The professional Toastmaster is trained in the protocol, craft and procedures of state, civic, corporate and social events. His genesis can be traced back to the staging of banquets of royal and noble households in the middle ages. He will be attired in a distinctive red uniform and will make scripted announcements in a formal manner. He will belong to a professional body, institute or collegiate guild who will have admitted him having achieved a required level of experience and standard of performance under examination.

The MC (Master of Ceremonies) on the other hand is not bound by any professional code of behaviour, has no specific uniform and delivers a performance in an informal style. The objectives of both types of performers are the same: to advise and guide guests, introduce speeches and entertainment and run an unrehearsed live event to a planned timetable. The nature of the event and wishes of the hosts determine which style will be appropriate. Toastmasters are able to adopt either persona or act as a hybrid as in 'firm but friendly'.

What should a couple look for in a Toastmaster?

The attributes a couple should look for in a Toastmaster are an engaging warm personality, a strong, clear, well-spoken voice that commands authority, a smart appearance, a knowledge of the customs, religious traditions and protocol of the wedding, relevant experience and membership of one of the respected professional Toastmaster organisations. Also important is to have confidence that the Toastmaster will be able to handle the unexpected.

What are the benefits of having a Toastmaster at an Asian wedding? Are toastmasters trained in the etiquettes of different Asian ceremonies?

A Toastmaster is an asset to any kind of wedding as its stage manager but particularly beneficial to Asian weddings which invariably involve large numbers of guests, colour, loud noise, spectacle and occasional chaos despite the most careful planning. There are centuries-old, sometimes long, often complicated ceremonies and rituals to introduce. There may be a 'western' civil wedding to handle on the same day as well. There will be multiple photographers and video cameramen with their lights and equipment. Often dhol players, musicians and sometimes Bollywood dancers are engaged. Catering is always a feast of many dishes or courses. Guests may not arrive on time and will be reluctant to remain quiet during speeches. Large groups of family members will want their photograph taking with the couple. There may be language problems and family sensitivities of which to be aware. With such a complex production, only the most experienced and calm Toastmaster will volunteer to manage the myriad of elements, many in conflict. It is essential he understands the basic ceremonies and customs at least of Hindu, Sikh and Muslim cultures and indeed if asked, can comfortably and authoritatively advise families on how they should be performed and what allowances should be made for timing, sequencing, effectiveness and issues about space.

How far in advance should you book a toastmaster?

Toastmasters are booked up to two years ahead, so it is never too early to engage one. It is advisable, if you can organise it, to meet with the prospective Toastmaster before commitment. Ask for testimonials from his previous client couples and then follow up by having a friendly chat with them.

What uniform do toastmasters wear?

A professional Toastmaster will by custom wear a red ('hunting pink') tailcoat over black trousers; around the neck will be a white bow tie, winged collar, white marcella shirt and waistcoat. This attire ensures he will stand out in a crowd of any size. Occasionally it may be preferred for the tailcoat to be a black one. It could also be requested for the Toastmaster to wear full Asian dress, shalwar kameez or similar. Whilst this may well be respectful, stylish and topical, the effect is to lose both the identity and with it the friendly authority of the Toastmaster among the guests and in diminishing his role, this style is therefore not recommended.

How far are most toastmasters willing to travel?

So long as English is the spoken language, most Toastmasters will travel anywhere in the world to perform their craft and it is always a great honour to be invited to participate. The principles of guest and event management are identical regardless of location or culture. Obviously, budgets need to accommodate the consequential extra demands of time and distance.

What are the duties of a Toastmaster at a Wedding Reception?

A Toastmaster's work at the venue starts one hour before any of the family or guests arrive, to check the elements are all in place or ready and that banqueting and technical staff are working to the same timetable. Some of the details on the Toastmaster's checklist will be: cloakrooms – are they open and clean? Test the microphones. Is the florist going to finish on time? Is the Mandap complete? Are there enough chairs? Is there reserved seating for close family and late-comers? What about the ramps for wheelchairs? Note position of the fire exits. How do the lighting and air-conditioning controls work? Has the cake (and knife) arrived? Table plans? Place cards? Favours? Photobooth? Liaising with photographers, videographers, the DJ, the Pandit or the Imam, as the eyes and ears of the couple, a Toastmaster will ensure all these items and more are, or will be, at the right place at the right time. A Toastmaster can also stage manage set piece moments, brief the guests in advance of what is about to happen, announce the speeches, the first dance, the entertainment, be on hand to answer questions, direct late arrivals and to help with seating and access.

What other duties can a Toastmaster carry out?

There should be no duty left to undertake or the Toastmaster would have overlooked an expectation so going the extra mile would involve a really good Toastmaster for example discreetly offering to assist the formal speakers with their material and if time permits, might listen to their rehearsal. The Toastmaster might also distribute payment to various artistes on behalf of the couple or take round the guest book for signing from table to table.

What is a receiving line?

A Receiving Line is where a group of hosts formally receive a line of guests who are announced by name by the Toastmaster after the wedding ceremony or 'going into the wedding breakfast'. The host group usually comprise (in this order) Mother of the Bride, Father of the Bride, Mother of the Groom, Father of the Groom, Bride and Groom. Guests are encouraged to keep moving, only to shake hands or kiss briefly and all are deterred from chatting. The perfect line should see guests move through at the rate of one every 10 seconds. A receiving line should not last longer than 30 minutes which suggests it should not be undertaken if guests number greater than 200. Because of the large numbers at Asian weddings and the unavailability of Bride and Groom at the most suitable moments, it is a rare feature.

How long do Toastmasters stay at a wedding?

The Toastmaster will stay until all the formal aspects have been completed and the dancing is underway with the DJ in control, unless of course there is to be a fireworks display or a helicopter departure, in which case guests will need to be advised, moved, guided and protected from danger!

HOW TO CONTACT US

Richard Birtchnell, The London Toastmaster Bookings and Enquiries:

Website: www.londontoastmaster.com

Email: info@londontoastmaster.com

Telephone: +44 (0)20 7730 3725

Fax: +44 (0)20 7730 1074

CONCLUSION

Congratulations! You now have the combined knowledge that all of our interviewees have been generous enough to share! We hope that you now feel confident and excited to go out and plan your special day. Before you get started, though, we'd just like to share a little more advice with you:

In all likelihood, you are only going to have one wedding. This also means that you're also only going to have one time in your life when you are planning your wedding. Our advice to you is to not make just the big day the only fun part. We truly hope that you enjoy the process of planning your wedding as much as you enjoy your wedding day.

All too often in life, we put all of our focus on the end result and we lose sight of the fact that the journey, not just the destination, should be exciting and enjoyable too. We hope that you find enjoyment in your wedding planning journey. We hope that you cherish each moment of planning your wedding, even if unexpected things still happen along the way. Always remember that life would be boring if everything always went exactly as expected. When unexpected things happen, try to smile and accept it as part of the journey.

We have done our best to compile the best advice that we were able to find, from true wedding industry professionals. Even though you now have a substantial advantage over couples who plan their weddings without the knowledge that you now have, there are still bound to be some bumps in the road, in the days leading up to your big day. As with all things in life, it's not what happens to you throughout the wedding planning process, it's how you handle those things that happen to you along the way. Embrace the challenges and welcome the unexpected. Each challenge that you resolve will bring you one step closer to your big day.

We wish you all the best as you plan your wedding. May you find happiness, excitement, and fun in all of the days leading up to your wedding, and beyond!

2842781R00069

Printed in Great Britain
by Amazon.co.uk, Ltd.,
Marston Gate.